CRITICAL STUDIES OF
KEY TEXTS

Charlotte Brontë's
Jane Eyre

CRITICAL STUDIES OF
KEY TEXTS

Charlotte Brontë's
Jane Eyre

Pauline Nestor

Monash University
Melbourne

St. Martin's Press
New York

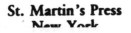

© Pauline Nestor, 1992
All rights reserved. For information, write
Scholarly and Reference Division,
St. Martin's Press, Inc., 175 Fifth Avenue, New York, NY 10010
First published in the United States of America in 1992
Printed in Great Britain
ISBN 0-312-08423-4 (cloth)   ISBN 0-312-08601-6 (paper)

Library of Congress Cataloging-in-Publication Data

Nestor, Pauline.
    Charlotte Brontë's Jane Eyre / by Pauline Nestor.
      p.   cm. – (Critical studies of key texts)
    ISBN 0-312-08423-4 (cloth). – ISBN 0-312-08601-6 (paper)
    1. Brontë, Charlotte, 1816–1855. Jane Eyre. I. Title.
II. Series.
PR4167.J5N47   1992
823′.8–dc20
                                92-17623
                                   CIP

Contents

I Contexts

Historical and Cultural Context   3
Critical Reception   12
Theoretical Perspectives   18

II Jane Eyre: A Reading of the Text

1. Motherhood   33
2. Sexuality   53
3. Identity   74
Conclusion   93

Notes   96
Select Bibliography   105
Index   111

I

Contexts

Historical and Cultural Context

In 1836 the 20-year-old Charlotte Brontë boldly sent her poetry to the Poet Laureate, Robert Southey, seeking his judgment. Southey's infamous reply urged her to forsake such unsuitable pursuits: 'Literature cannot be the business of a woman's life, and it ought not to be. The more she is engaged in her proper duties, the less leisure will she have for it, even as an accomplishment and a recreation'.[1] Sixteen years later, as Brontë was struggling with the final chapters of her fourth novel, *Villette*, George Lewes, in the pages of the *Westminster Review*, could confidently welcome the 'appearance of Woman in the field of literature'.[2] Whatever we may conclude from this about the respective sympathies of the two men or about the brave perseverance of Brontë in her determination to be an author, what the juxtaposition points to most of all is the pace of change for women during Brontë's lifetime.

Brontë died too early to witness most of the changes that were to come, though she knew at first hand many of the constraints suffered by women in mid-nineteenth-century England. Her formal education, for example, was limited and sporadic – ten months at the age of 8 at Cowan Bridge charity school (the model for Lowood school in *Jane Eyre*), eighteen months from the age of 14 at Miss Wooler's school at Roe Head, and less than two years from the age of 25 at the Pensionnat Heger in Brussels, paid for by a loan from her aunt and by her services there as a teacher. Even such modest schooling was provided at the cost of considerable sacrifice to her family and was undertaken by Charlotte with the determination to make the most of what was offered, spurred on by the knowledge that in time 'she must provide for herself' (*LL*, I, 92): 'She always seemed to feel that a deep responsibility rested upon her; that she was an object of expense to those at home, and that she must use every moment to attain the purpose for which she was sent to school, *i.e.*, to fit herself for governess life' (*LL*, I, 94).

While Brontë's formal education was frustratingly limited, the comparatively unconventional circumstances of her upbringing allowed her an unusual degree of latitude in her private pursuit of learning. Through a combination of enlightenment and neglect, her father Patrick Brontë gave virtual free rein to his children's reading. Charlotte avidly read contemporary newspapers and magazines, and was as familiar with the comedies of Shakespeare and the poetry of Byron as she was with the Bible and *The Pilgrim's Progress*. She also found time for her own prolific juvenile output, for though she was required to help with domestic tasks, her time was not as relentlessly supervised and consumed by mindless pastimes as that of many of the daughters of the middle class. Furthermore, unlike many of her middle-class sisters, Brontë was not made to feel the compulsion to marry. She grew up with a healthy respect for female autonomy – 'there is no more respectable character on this earth than an unmarried woman who makes her way quietly perseveringly' (*LL*, II, 77) – and she regarded dependence as the 'one great curse of a single female life' (*LL*, III, 5). In the isolation of Haworth, under the care of her harsh but spirited maiden aunt and her eccentric father, she was spared the machinations of the 'marriage market' where, she recognised, women 'reared on speculation with a view to their making mercenary marriages' were 'piteously degraded' (*LL*, II, 221).

While the necessity to work at least spared Brontë the mindless indolence of fashionable feminine existence, she was none the less faced with the painful fact that for a woman of her class the only occupation open to her in 1835 was some form of what she termed 'governessing slavery'. Temperamentally unsuited to such an occupation, she was miserable in her years as an assistant teacher at Miss Wooler's school, and she resigned to return home a 'shattered wretch' in May 1838. In the following years she took up two governessing positions, though she claimed to '*hate* and *abhor* the very thought of governesship' (*LL*, I, 194), the 'living in other people's houses – the estrangement from one's real character' (*LL*, I, 241). The one ray of light for Charlotte at this time was her plan to open her own school, a scheme which seemed to satisfy her own desire for autonomy and the problems arising from Anne's poor health, Emily's chronic homesickness and the daughters' abiding preoccupation with the care of their father. However, even with the language skills acquired in Brussels, she was never able to attract sufficient students to mount the venture.

The prospects for a gentlewoman like Brontë, then, were bleak: 'I shall soon be 30', she wrote in 1845, 'I have done nothing yet. . . . There was a time when Haworth was a very pleasant place to me, it is not so now – I feel as if we were all buried here – I long to travel – to work to live a life of action' (*LL*, II, 28). Brontë's horizons were, of course, set to expand dramatically. Within three years she had published, with her sisters, the unsuccessful *Poems* by Acton, Ellis and Currer Bell, seen her first novel, *The Professor*, repeatedly rejected by a succession of publishers, and been catapulted into literary celebrity with the publication of *Jane Eyre*, one of the best-sellers of 1847.

Brontë's new career brought her an extraordinary degree of autonomy – the £500 she earned for *Jane Eyre* represented twenty-five times the annual salary of her last governessing position, and the fame that accompanied her literary triumph opened many doors. Yet even as one of the most successful writers of her day, the conditions under which she pursued her career were circumscribed by her gender. She adopted a pseudonym at the outset because she rightly feared the critical double standards that operated against women: 'we had a vague impression that authoresses are liable to be looked on with prejudice; we noticed how critics sometimes use for their chastisement the weapon of personality, and for their reward a flattery which is not true praise' (*LL*, II, 80). Similarly, her success as an author was never allowed to displace her 'proper duties', the demands on her as a daughter. Even her friend and fellow author Elizabeth Gaskell did not question the justice of the 'double time' – domestic and professional – that Brontë was compelled to serve:

> When a man becomes an author, it is probably merely a change of employment to him. . . . But no other can take up the quiet, regular duties of the daughter, the wife, or the mother, as well as she whom God has appointed to fill that particular place: a woman's principal work in life is hardly left to her own choice; nor can she drop the domestic charges devolving on her as an individual, for the exercise of the most splendid talents that were ever bestowed. And yet she must not shrink from the extra responsibility implied by the very fact of her possessing such talents.[3]

In 1854 Charlotte Brontë married the Reverend Arthur Nicholls. She found her life 'changed indeed', as her writing virtually ceased and she took up the duties of a minister's wife. In accordance with the expectations of her time, she became a 'helpmeet' to her husband while still the dutiful daughter to her father, occupying the private sphere of home and hearth and leaving the public realm to him. In many ways, then, the last two years of Brontë's life exemplified the doctrine of two spheres which was extensively articulated in Ruskin's *Sesame and Lilies*, for example, and which opposed a private feminine world to a public masculine one. In such a scheme woman's virtue was seen as inherent, not achieved – she did not so much exercise piety and restraint as embody innocence and purity. In consequence, qualities and characteristics were represented as natural, when in fact, as John Stuart Mill pointed out, they were clearly political and culturally constructed.[4]

Charlotte Brontë had refused three proposals before agreeing to marry Nicholls, a fact that contradicts Thackeray's demeaning portrait of her emotional desperation: 'rather than have fame, rather than any other earthly good or mayhap heavenly one, she wants some Tomkins or another to love her and be in love with'.[5] In her acceptance of Nicholls, however, there was more a sense of resignation than enthusiasm, born perhaps of her painful loneliness after the death of her three siblings. And in her talk of 'esteem' and affection, 'if not love' (*LL*, IV, 112), there is no suggestion of the sexual desire which her heroines so defiantly demonstrated and her age so steadfastly denied. The constriction of female costume, the celebration in art of the enervated female form, the displacement in fiction of the sexual on to familial bonding, the revival in poetry and art of medievalism, with its chivalric code which objectified women as chaste and untouchable – all attested to the subversion and denial of female sexuality in mid-nineteenth-century England.

In the same year as Brontë's marriage, the young activist Barbara Leigh Smith issued her *Brief Statement in Plain Language of the Most Important Laws Concerning Women*. The pamphlet outlined the legal effacement of women in marriage: 'A man and wife are one person in law; the wife loses all her rights as a single woman, and her existence is entirely absorbed in that of her husband.'[6] For Brontë, as for all married women, not merely her personal wealth but her very body became the property of her husband. Similarly, any children or subsequent earnings would belong to her husband. Having lost any 'separate existence' under law, she could not enter contracts or be punished for a range of offences committed in her husband's presence or against his person. In effect, she was deemed legally no more responsible than a child or a lunatic. (Interestingly, under the law as it stood at the time of Brontë's writing *Jane Eyre*, Bertha Mason could never have been prosecuted for setting fire to Thornfield. Her immunity would be based not on her madness but on the fact that as Rochester's wife she was regarded as 'one person in law' and thus could not be seen as having acted against him.)

Charlotte Brontë was fully aware of such 'evils', but thought them 'deep-rooted in the foundations of the social system – which no efforts of ours can touch; of which we cannot complain; of which it is advisable not too often to think'

7

(*LL*, III, 150). None the less, she did speak out in her fiction about the intellectual and spiritual equality of women, the degrading restrictions on women's employment and the validity of women's sexual desire, thus making what Geoffrey Tillotson has called 'her chief contribution to the public thought of her time'.[7] And while Brontë might personally have eschewed activism, she was frankly admiring of her activist friend Mary Taylor, one of many women working in a growing movement for change, whom Brontë declared had 'more energy and power in her nature than any ten men you can pick out in the united parishes of Birstall and Gomersal' (*LL*, I, 223).

In her lifetime Brontë saw the beginnings of a feminist movement. As more and more women became politicised through their involvement in philanthropy and in a variety of movements ranging from Chartism and the Anti-Corn Law League to abolitionism, their agitation focused particularly on demands for female suffrage, reform of the marriage laws, and expanded opportunities for women's education and employment. Though Brontë did not live to experience the gains in educational and employment opportunities that followed soon after her death, she did at least enjoy the celebrity and respect that accompanied the increasingly 'prominent position in the field of literature' accorded women novelists.[8]

Brontë's was a particularly literary life – from her earliest years, reading and writing were centrally important to her. As Mary Taylor confirmed, 'artists and authors stood high with Charlotte' (*LL*, I, 276), and by the age of 14 Charlotte could proudly list an extraordinary array of tales, plays, poems and romances written in the previous fifteen months, making 'in the whole twenty-two volumes'.[9] Despite this, however, she held earlier novelists in fairly low esteem. She had reserved respect for George Sand, for example, but was resolutely unimpressed by Jane Austen: 'She does the business of delineating the surface of the lives of genteel English people curiously well . . . [but] the Passions are perfectly unknown to her' (*LL*, III, 99). In devising a reading list for her friend Ellen Nussey in 1834 she recommended lists of poets, biographers and historians, but declared that for fiction Ellen should 'read Scott alone; all novels after his are worthless' (*LL*, I, 122).[10] Amongst her contemporaries she admired Thackeray above all, and expressed respect for the skill of both Harriet Martineau and Elizabeth Gaskell. In all, though, she firmly disclaimed any literary debt:

> The standard heroes and heroines of novels are personages in whom I could never from childhood upwards take an interest, believe to be natural, or wish to imitate. Were I obliged to copy any former novelist, even the greatest, even Scott, in anything, I would not write. Unless I have something of my own to say, and a way of my own to say it in, I have no business to publish. Unless I can look beyond the great Masters, and study Nature herself, I have no right to paint. Unless I have the courage to use the language of Truth in preference to the jargon of conventionality, I ought to be silent. (*LL*, II, 255)

Such a claim is, of course, at once grand and naïve in its assumption that her writing could somehow emerge fully formed and untouched by her cultural milieu.[11] In general Brontë's work seems poised between a Romantic heritage and a Victorian future. Not only do her heroes show signs of her abiding admiration for Byron, but her preoccupation with the individual quest, and with the authority of the imagination and feeling, link her strongly with a Romantic past. Against this, however, Brontë demonstrates a more distinctively Victorian realism, stressing the plainness of her protagonists, the harsh and obstructive reality of material circumstance, and the need to reconcile both the individual to the social and the impulses of Feeling to the dictates of Reason. Similarly, she makes use of some aspects of earlier Gothic writing, but once again she modifies the form, as Robert Heilman argues, to imbue it with a new symbolic and psychological resonance.[12]

More particularly, the influence of Walter Scott can be found in the sweep of historical romance in the juvenilia, the mark of Samuel Richardson has been noted in Brontë's creation of entrapped heroines and lengthy internal monologues,[13] and the contemporary influence of Thackeray is suggested in the narrative voice and scope of *Shirley*. Further,

Jane Eyre has been suggestively linked with the conventions of fictional 'autobiography', especially in the works of Godwin, Lytton and Disraeli.[14]

Perhaps the clearest formative influence for Brontë, though, was the most local – her life at Haworth Parsonage, which provided her with the religious reading evident in the consistent echoes in her work of the Bible, Bunyan, *Paradise Lost*, Isaac Watts, and the rhetoric of the religious quest. It also provided her with the crucial collaboration of her siblings. Her juvenilia were produced in close association with her brother Branwell, and in the earlier part of her mature writing career she shared an enabling sense of *esprit de corps* with her sisters Emily and Anne.

Both Anne and Emily had written their first novels before Charlotte wrote *Jane Eyre*, and their influence could account in some part for the improvement from *The Professor* to *Jane Eyre*. The first-person female narration of *Agnes Grey* may have prompted Charlotte, who had never used a female narrator in any of her juvenilia, to change from the uneasily rendered male narrator of *The Professor* to the powerful female voice of *Jane Eyre*. Similarly, the poetic force of Emily's prose and the passionate, supernatural bond between Emily's lovers arguably found some echo in the relationship between Jane and Rochester and the increased emphasis on a connection between Charlotte's heroine and the natural world. The importance of Charlotte's two sisters to her literary endeavour is evident, too, in the fact that after their deaths she found herself more vulnerable to criticism and less confident in her judgment, as an author 'who has shewn his book to none, held no consultation about plan, subject, character or incidents, asked and had no opinion from one living being, but fabricated it darkly in the silent workshop of his own brain' (*LL*, III, 21).

Whatever Brontë's literary debt, her legacy to the novel was profound. In her six short years of novel-writing she established an authority that was rivalled only by George Eliot. Reviewers and critics of the period attest to her decisive influence on the conception of the Victorian heroine, and her contemporary, the novelist Margaret Oliphant, claimed that 'no other writer of her time has impressed her mark so clearly on contemporary literature, or drawn so many followers onto her peculiar path'.[15]

Critical Reception

After the dismal failure of her first publishing venture, *Poems* by Currer, Ellis and Acton Bell, which sold only two copies, Charlotte Brontë could scarcely have dreamed of the scale of success that awaited *Jane Eyre*. On its appearance in October 1847 the work met with immediate critical and popular acclaim. The influential critic George Lewes declared it 'the best novel of the season',[16] and the *Atlas* deemed it 'not merely a work of great promise; it is one of absolute performance' (*CH*, 67). The novel had run to three editions within six months, with *The Times* estimating its admirers in the millions (*CH*, 151) and one American critic describing its hold on the public as ' "Jane Eyre fever" ' (*CH*, 97).

Amidst the initial 'near unanimity of praise', certain features of the novel were consistently commended. It was repeatedly hailed as 'fresh', 'original' and 'vigorous', and – perhaps more surprisingly to modern eyes – celebrated for its realism. So, *Fraser's Magazine* claimed that the work was characterised by 'deep, significant reality' (*CH*, 84), while *Blackwood's Magazine* thought it 'so like truth that it is difficult to avoid believing that much of the characters and incidents are taken from life' (*CH*, 95). The reviewer for *Putnam's Monthly Magazine* suggested that the novel demonstrated an '*actuality*' typical of the 'very genius and spirit of modern English fiction' (*CH*, 213).

Although they were overwhelmingly favourable, many of the early reviews contained within them the seeds of more negative criticism. The reviewers' gradual shift in emphasis from positive to negative was prompted, at least in part, by a damaging association with Anne's controversial *The Tenant of Wildfell Hall*, which appeared in the summer of 1848, and it culminated in Elizabeth Rigby's virulent attack in the *Quarterly Review* in December 1848. What had been passing reservations concerning the 'crudeness of youth', the 'rude and uncultivated [style] here and there' and 'faults on the side of vigour' became an increasingly prevalent theme in the criticism of Charlotte's work in the early 1850s – to the point where Elizabeth Gaskell was particularly anxious about the posthumous publication of *The Professor*, 'For I would not, if I could help it, have another syllable that could be called coarse to be associated with her name' (*CH*, 320).

This increasing preoccupation with the novel's 'coarseness' was one manifestation of the sexist double standards operating in the criticism of the day, which Brontë had unsuccessfully sought to avoid in adopting a pseudonym. A prescriptive set of assumptions about womanly behaviour and capability led to the designation of the novel's 'vigour' and its 'power, breadth and shrewdness' as 'masculine' or 'over-masculine', and to apprehension at the possibility that Brontë's style might degenerate into vulgarities that would be 'inexcusable – even in a man' (*CH*, 165). When the *Christian Remembrancer* declared of *Jane Eyre* that it would be hard to find a book in the annals of female authorship 'more unfeminine both in its excellences and defects' (*CH*, 89), Charlotte Brontë was damned both ways – in her defects she failed her sex, and in her excellences she transcended it.

Despite such double standards, the prospects of contemporary success for *Jane Eyre* were enhanced by the fact that it appeared during something of a hiatus in the development of the novel. Accordingly, it was greeted by the *People's Journal* as 'quite a relief to find a really good and striking production. English "fiction" is *not* entirely a "fraud", as we were beginning to suspect' (*CH*, 80); and Lewes, in the *Edinburgh Review*, declared: 'it is certain that, for many years, there had been no work of such power, piquancy and originality' (*CH*, 163). When the *Era* declared that the work was 'without rival among modern productions', the stature of the opposition was scarcely overwhelming: 'Bulwer, [G.P.R.] James, D'Israeli, and all the serious novel writers of the day lose in comparison with Currer Bell' (*CH*, 79). The notoriety of the novel was further enhanced by an extraordinary preoccupation with the mystery surrounding its authorship and subsequently by the arresting details of the Brontë biography.

The novel's lasting success can be partly attributed to another feature which preoccupied admiring and hostile reviewers alike – that is, the work's articulation of rebellion, which is given power and directness in the skilful execution of the first-person narrative, and its satisfying, fable-like vision of fulfilment. Even those who saw *Jane Eyre* as a 'dangerous book' indirectly paid compliment to the deep chord of sympathy it struck in so many readers. Thus it was its subversive power, its 'moral Jacobinism' (*CH*, 90), that most outraged Elizabeth Rigby:

> there is that pervading tone of ungodly discontent which is at once the most prominent and the most subtle evil which the law and the pulpit, which all civilized society in fact has at the present to contend with. We do not hesitate to say that the tone of the mind and thought which has overthrown authority and violated every code human and divine abroad, and fostered Chartism and rebellion at home, is the same which has also written Jane Eyre. (*CH*, 110)

From the Continent Eugène Forçade judged that the novel's 'accent of revolt' and 'aspirations to independence' frightened conservative critics (*CH*, 143), and Margaret Oliphant, while characterising *Jane Eyre* as 'a wild declaration of the "Rights of Woman" in a new aspect', conceded that 'the doctrines, startling and original, propounded by Jane Eyre . . . are not Jane Eyre's opinions only, as we may guess from the host of followers or imitators who have copied them' (*CH*, 313).

The success of *Villette* in 1853, Charlotte's death in 1855, and the interest and sympathy aroused by subsequent biographical notices, especially Elizabeth Gaskell's *Life of Charlotte Brontë* in 1857, ensured that Brontë continued to receive critical attention throughout the 1850s. However, Peter Bayne was wrong on two counts when, in 1857, he confidently predicted: 'It may be doubted whether any more than a faint and mournful reminiscence of Ellis and Acton Bell will survive the generation now passing away. But the case is widely different with the eldest of the sisters. Currer Bell has won for herself a place in our literature from which she cannot be deposed' (*CH*, 326). Throughout the 1860s, with George Eliot's star clearly on the horizon, Brontë received comparatively scant attention, and the following decade saw the beginning of a trend in which the critical estimation of Charlotte was invariably linked in inverse relation to that of Emily, with Emily's reputation largely in the ascendant for the next eighty years.

The 1870s saw fresh editions of Charlotte's novels and a biography by T. W. Reid. More importantly for Brontë's critical standing, they also saw an extravagantly laudatory essay by Algernon Swinburne and a reply by Leslie Stephen in 1877. Swinburne's essay was an attempt to reverse the critical tide running in favour of George Eliot and re-establish 'the genius of Charlotte Brontë' (*CH*, 406). However, Leslie Stephen, countering Swinburne's eulogy, called for careful analysis, arguing the need for 'scientific method' rather than excessive 'oratorical impulse'. Stephen acknowledged Brontë's 'high' place in the 'great hierarchy of imaginative authors', and had no time for the earlier moralism of the 'luckless critics who blundered so hopelessly in failing to recognize' her 'instinctive nobility of spirit'. None the less he criticised Brontë's earnestness, her 'comparative narrowness', and the 'feverish disquiet' that disrupted her prose, and he regretted the lack of a more powerful intellect that 'would even under her conditions have worked out some more comprehensive and harmonious solution' (*CH*, 422). Suggesting that subjectivity was the mark of inferior art, Stephen made a decisive and reductive connection between Brontë's life and writing, claiming that her characters were 'more or less mouthpieces' and her experience was 'scarcely transformed in passing through her mind'. Indeed, in declaring 'the study of her life is the study of her novels', he succinctly revealed the simplistic conflation underlying much of the Brontë criticism before and since. Even more importantly, in setting up ideals of objectivity and detachment, unity, harmony and decisiveness, Stephen provided a set of criteria against which Brontë's novels were judged to be lacking for the next eighty years (*CH*, 413–23).

Mary Ward, for example, in her introductions to the Haworth edition of the Brontës' work (1899–1900), claimed that 'personality' was the 'sole but sufficient spell' of Charlotte's novels, and accepted Stephen's assessment of Brontë's narrowness. Similarly, Lord David Cecil dealt a body blow to Charlotte's reputation in 1934 when he characterised her works as unreflectively subjective, 'not exercises of the mind, but cries of the heart; not a deliberate self-diagnosis, but an involuntary self-revelation', and concluded, like Stephen, that they lacked 'artistic unity'.[17] Even Virginia Woolf, in *A Room of One's Own* (1928), betrayed echoes of her father, Leslie Stephen, when she regretted the 'rancour which contracts these books, splendid as they are, with a spasm of pain'.[18] Subsequently, F. R. Leavis not only excluded Charlotte from his 'great tradition' in 1948, but in claiming that it was 'tempting to retort there is only one Brontë [Emily]',[19] he confirmed the tendency to value Emily at Charlotte's expense which had already been demonstrated by Mary Ward and David Cecil.

The development of New Criticism in the 1940s and 1950s created the possibility at least that the discussion of Charlotte Brontë might escape the reductive conflation of author with character and biography with fiction which had dogged the critical reception of her novels. Although the New Critics were in general far more interested in poetry than in the realist novel and Brontë's fiction was in any case not especially conducive to readings determined, as New Criticism was, to sever the author completely from the text, textual studies influenced by New Criticism did begin to reorientate the assessments of her artistry.

Nevertheless, in 1960 D. W. Crompton could still claim that

there was a critical consensus on the comparatively minor significance of Charlotte Brontë's novels: 'one is still left with the fact (which cannot be argued here but is at least generally accepted) that *Wuthering Heights* is a great book and that *Jane Eyre* — whatever its structure — is relatively miniature in conception and execution and yields little more from sustained consideration than it does from a single reading.'[20] Since Crompton's pronouncement, however, the last three decades have seen a marked resurgence of interest in and appreciation of Charlotte Brontë's work, the theoretical implications of which will be explored in the next section.

Theoretical Perspectives

No single theoretical perspective has been responsible for the resurgence in Charlotte Brontë's critical reputation in the last thirty years. Rather, Brontë's work, and *Jane Eyre* in particular, has provided fertile ground for a variety of critical approaches – most notably psychoanalytic, feminist, Marxist and an 'intrinsic' or textually based criticism informed by a spectrum of approaches, ranging from New Criticism and formalism to structuralism and post-structuralism.

The early New Critical and formalist analyses were defined by their reaction against the excessively biographical, heavily subjective studies which Robert Martin, in his book *The Accents of Persuasion: Charlotte Brontë's novels* (1966), dubbed 'The Purple Heather School of Criticism and Biography'. These studies explicitly challenged earlier dismissive assessments of Brontë's fiction. They characteristically offered close, sustained textual analyses and emphasised the artistry of Brontë's work in order to show, as Earl A. Knies contended, that 'she is more than the inspired improviser and fictionalised autobiographer that she was long considered to be'.[21] Knies was typical of these critics in his determination to 'read the novels as coherent fictions' without recourse to biography or historical context. In *The Cover of the Mask: The autobiographers in Charlotte Brontë's fiction* (1982), for example, Annette Tromly is critical both of studies which canvass the novels 'for undigested traces of Brontë's experience' and of those that 'mine' them for evidence of Brontë's religious beliefs, social values and feminist politics: 'As Brontë the apologist replaces Brontë the sufferer, then, Brontë the creator continues to elude us.'[22] Tromly, like Earl Knies, stresses the inadequacy and unreliability of Brontë biography, and shifts the focus to the 'process of aesthetic transformation'.

In rejecting biography, however, these studies have not rejected a notion of authorial identity. On the contrary, their stress on the artistry of Brontë's fiction implicitly posits a conscious, authoritative creative presence. It is true that more recent textual studies, drawing on post-structuralist theory, are unlikely to accept the transcendent authority of the author, but they are equally drawn through close textual analysis to the examination of the tensions and divisions so characteristic of the novel, variously manifest as the opposition between reason and feeling, romance and realism, grace and nature, inclusion and exclusion, and the doubling of opposed characters such as Helen and Bertha, Rochester and St John, the three wicked Reed cousins and the three good Rivers cousins. Despite this shared focus, there remains a difference of emphasis. New Critical and formalist studies tend to celebrate balance and fusion – as, for example, in Robert Martin's claim that while the play of Charlotte Brontë's imagination 'achieves many of its finest effects by lurid contrasts', in *Jane Eyre* 'for the first time Charlotte Brontë has the imaginative, comprehensive grasp of her material that manages to fuse its disparate parts into a real unity'.[23] Post-structuralist studies, in contrast, tend to foreground division and contradiction, as in Richard Benevenuto's contention that the novel reveals the absence of any pattern by which the two competing value systems of nature and grace can be harmonised:

> But nature and grace do not make relative claims upon Jane. They stand for two self-identities, for forces inclusive of her whole being, which is divided so completely that two self-images claim possession of all her human faculties. . . . Not one unitive personality with different parts to it, but two unitive personalities contesting against each other make up her character.[24]

This difference of emphasis between formalist studies extends to the perception of methodology. Thus structuralist contributions to narrative theory foreground the attempt to isolate the 'grammar' of the plot and to identify the codes or systems of figures and conventions which produce meaning in narrative, and have been used fruitfully, for example, to explore the powerful shaping consciousness of Brontë's first-person narrative in *Jane Eyre*. So, Peter Allan Dale contends that every narrative 'initiates certain expectations because it is in some significant degree derived from a code or grammar of narratology with which the "competent reader" is familiar'; and in this light he goes on to examine Brontë as the 'master of suspended expectation'.[25] Narrative codes similarly preoccupy Annette Tromly, who stresses that Brontë's novels are not 'autobiography cast in fictional form' but 'fictions cast in what Brontë called "the autobiographic form"', and explores the 'distortions of self-portraiture'.[26] Tony Tanner's approach in 'Passion, narrative and identity in *Wuthering Heights* and *Jane Eyre*' (1983), while equally concerned with the narrative act, is without scientific pretension. From a position which reflects the New Critical perception of literature as a 'form of human understanding',[27] Tanner examines the way in which Jane Eyre has literally 'to create herself in writing' so that the narrative act becomes 'an act of self-definition'. Tanner sees Jane's artistry, her 'gift for narrative', as transcendent, 'larger than the very constricted compass of her actual social existence'.[28]

Margot Peters falls somewhere between the scientific and humanist positions with her book *Charlotte Brontë: Style in the novel* (1973). Peters seeks explicitly 'to reconcile the precision and objectivity of linguistic analysis with the more intuitive and interpretative discipline of literary criticism'. She sees this meeting-ground in stylistics, and attempts 'a scientific study of style', analysing, for example, Brontë's characteristic use of antithesis and inversion.[29]

The limitations of these 'intrinsic', textual analyses are consciously chosen and articulated. They offer very little contextual examination of the text because they start from the premiss that, as Karl Kroeber argues, the arts 'possess a history of their own' which is 'to some degree independent of, often surprisingly resistant to, the influence of social transformations'.[30] In this sense they may consider developments within a genre, as Robert Heilman does in his influential study of the way in which Brontë imbues Gothic devices with a new pychological resonance and force,[31] but they limit their attention to the 'intrinsic processes' or 'aesthetic systems' of the work of art. As a consequence, these kinds of reading tend to be politically neutralising, denying the pervasive operation of ideology which is so central, for example, to feminist and Marxist critiques.

While one strand of Brontë criticism has eschewed biographical concerns, the details of the Brontë lives have never ceased to exert a certain fascination for another group of readers and critics. Accordingly, Brontë criticism has long been influenced by a psychoanalytic perspective, from the pre-Freudian, amateur interpretation of Mrs Gaskell's 1857 *Life of Charlotte Brontë* to the more explicitly professional analysis of Lucile Dooley's 1920 article in the *American Journal of Psychology*, 'Psychoanalysis of Charlotte Brontë as a type of the woman of genius', or Rosamond Langbridge's 1934 work, *Charlotte Brontë: A psychological study*. More recently, psychoanalytic interpretations have taken a variety of forms. In some studies psychological theory is applied exclusively to the author's work. In '*Jane Eyre*: The quest for optimism' (1988), for example, Frederick Ashe regards the text almost as source material for a case study: 'The medical implications of the Red Room incident run perhaps even deeper than Bernstein allows, as Jane's emotional reaction provides a textbook example of mental depression.'[32]

In contrast, studies such as Helene Moglen's *Charlotte Brontë: The self conceived* (1976) and Robert Keefe's *Charlotte Brontë's World of Death* (1979) have considered biography and literary criticism jointly, regarding the interaction of life and literature as 'the critical element'. Both studies focus on the trauma of mother-loss, but while Keefe views Brontë's life more in terms of individual neurosis, Moglen links Brontë's experience more broadly to the situation of women, relating her growth to 'formations of the modern female psyche' and seeing it as indicative of 'the nature of the feminist struggle'.[33] Similarly, Irene Tayler has continued this psychological investigation of the link between life and literature in her book *Holy Ghosts: The male muses of Emily and Charlotte Brontë* (1990), which examines the creative development of the two sisters in relation to their creation of a male muse. Tayler argues that despite differences in their attitude to maleness and femaleness, Charlotte and Emily 'shared fully the view that the essential characteristic of femaleness was "being", of maleness, "doing"; and each saw in herself both male and female elements'.[34] Tayler sees Charlotte as profoundly divided between a desire to be loved by a creative and charismatic man, and, at the same time, a desire to be creative and charismatic herself. The solution to her dilemma is achieved only in the last years in her fiction, according to Tayler, where she was able to imagine 'a male figure who could both love the woman in her and at the same time arouse, encourage, and redeem her "masculine" powers'.[35]

Such criticism is at best illuminating and suggestive, but it remains of necessity highly speculative and, as Annette Tromly points out, provides only 'a variation – albeit a highly stimulating one – on Leslie Stephen's position'.[36] There is perhaps at times not all that much difference between the nineteenth-century use of the life to pity Brontë and the twentieth-century use to pathologise her.

Karen Chase also makes use of a psychoanalytic perspective in her book *Eros and Psyche: The representation of personality in Charlotte Brontë, Charles Dickens and George Eliot* (1984), but she does not focus on the author's life. Rather, she combines psychoanalysis with structuralist principles to investigate simultaneously the 'aesthetic and psychological' dimensions of Brontë's 'fictive representation of personality'. Chase is more concerned with the 'expressive' structure of *Jane Eyre* than with its 'narrative' or 'thematic' structure. Thus she explores its technique for organising 'certain permanent issues of emotional experience: such as the relations of power and victimage, desire and restraint, guilt and innocence'. She characterises her approach as one that regards the work as 'an affective whole, a global configuration of forces, tensions, evasions, suppressions, displacements, and compromises'.[37]

A further productive application of psychoanalysis has been made primarily by feminist critics who, drawing on strategies of post-structuralism and deconstruction, read the text not simply thematically but also symptomatically, alert to the workings of a 'textual unconscious'. So, rather than simply applying psychological theory to a work, these critics seek to psychoanalyse the text itself. Mary Poovey, for example, highlights the symptoms of repression in *Jane Eyre* in *Uneven Developments: The ideological work of gender in mid-Victorian England*:

> In the sense that narrative effect is split off from psychological cause, *Jane Eyre* becomes at these moments, what we might call a hysterical text, in which the body of the text symptomatically acts out what cannot make its way into the psychologically realistic narrative. Because there was no permissible plot in the nineteenth century for a woman's anger, whenever Brontë explores this form of self-assertion the text splinters hysterically, provoked by and provoking images of dependence and frustration.[38]

In the last two decades the most fruitful theoretical challenge to readings of Brontë's work have come from Marxism and, even more importantly, from feminism. Significantly, neither approach represents a single mode of inquiry in itself; rather, each draws on a range of other criticisms in order to identify the ideological structures of the text and what they reveal of the relation of literature to the social order. In this sense both have worked to recontextualise the text in opposition to the ahistorical perspective of the New Critics and structuralists. In line with the work of Michel Foucault and Edward Said, both approaches recognise the 'worldliness' of the text – that is, its inextricable relation to social and political struggle.

Marxist critiques of *Jane Eyre* tend to focus on the novel's 'deep divisions', which are regarded as symptomatic of the work's conflicting ideologies. So, for example, Terry Eagleton has argued that *Jane Eyre* should be read as a 'myth' that attempts to fuse irreconcilable elements of 'blunt bourgeois rationality and flamboyant Romanticism . . . passionate rebellion and cautious conformity', and that its structural dividedness embodies 'a complex structure of convergence and antagonism between the landed and industrial sectors of the contemporary ruling class'.[39] Similarly, Jina Politi, in '*Jane Eyre* class-ified', argues that, contrary to conscious intention, Jane and her narrative together grow 'from revolted marginality to quiescent socialization, reblending the contradictions which it initially exposed, thus securing its survival through the convention of a "happy ending". Revolution will bend to capitulation and the text will celebrate the very ideology which it set out to expose.'[40] Politi's reading adds the dimension of gender to that of class – a crucial conjunction according to the Marxist–Feminist Literature Collective, who criticise Eagleton's 'reductionist' reading of Jane Eyre as an 'asexual representative of the upwardly-mobile bourgeoisie'.[41] They contend that it is only a 'synthesis' of Marxist and psychoanalytic thought that can expose 'the crucial inter-dependence between class structure and patriarchy'.[42]

Of all the developments in critical theory, the emergence of feminist criticism in the last twenty-five years has had the most decisive effect on the critical perception of Charlotte Brontë. In this time feminist criticism has repeatedly demonstrated its capacity to invest the critic with 'fresh eyes' with which 'to enter an old text from a new critical direction'.[43] Such feminist 're-vision' has taken place on a number of fronts. It has given rise, for example, to a recognition of the importance of interdisciplinary study for an understanding of the sociohistorical context in which the Brontës produced their novels. So, Harriet Bjork has analysed Brontë's response to contemporary social thought in *The Language of Truth: Charlotte Brontë, the woman question, and the novel* (1974), and Françoise Basch has explored the social context of representations of women in *Relative Creatures: Victorian women in society and the novel 1837–67* (1974). More generally, pioneering work in an effort to chart a female literary tradition and to see the Brontës' work as part of that continuing tradition has been done by critics such as Inga-Stina Ewbank in *Their Proper Sphere: A study of the Brontë sisters as early Victorian novelists* (1966), Vineta Colby in *The Singular Anomaly: Women novelists of the nineteenth century* (1970), Ellen Moers in *Literary Women* (1976) and Elaine Showalter in *A Literature of Their Own: British women novelists from Brontë to Lessing* (1977).

Feminist criticism has also contributed a more complex and controversial sense of the qualities of women's writing. On the one hand, critics like Mary Ellmann in *Thinking About Women* (1968) have challenged stereotypes of feminine form-lessness, irrationality, spirituality, and the like. On the other, some feminist critics have sought to explore the distinctive qualities of women's prose and give to 'the idea of *difference* a new and positive force'.[44] The result has been a stimulating controversy over feminine aesthetics, and the efforts of some critics – such as Sandra Gilbert and Susan Gubar in *The Madwoman in the Attic: The woman writer and the nineteenth-century literary imagination* (1979) – to analyse the qualities of the female imagination. The subtitle of Gilbert and Gubar's book indicates the scope and ambition of the work. It seeks to identify the common features of women's writing in the nine-teenth century, and in its endeavour to outline a 'feminist poetics', *The Madwoman* represents a significant advance in theoretical sophistication for feminist literary criticism. Gilbert and Gubar argue that the absence of literary 'mothers' for women writers in the nineteenth century exposes the inadequacy of Harold Bloom's 'anxiety of influence' as a theory of women's literary creativity. They conclude that in a culture that defined creativity as masculine, women writers suffered instead from a debilitating 'anxiety of authorship'. As a consequence, women have produced strategically duplicitous works, as though heeding Emily Dickinson's advice to 'Tell all the Truth but tell it slant'. Gilbert and Gubar read nineteenth-century women's texts, then, as 'palimpsestic', presenting a surface which disguises 'less accessible (and less socially accept-able) levels of meaning', and thus managing 'the difficult task of achieving true female literary authority by simultaneously conforming to and subverting patriarchal literary standards'.[45] In brilliantly highlighting the importance of the subversive subtext in women's writing, Gilbert and Gubar were instru-mental in opening up one of the most fruitful areas of feminist literary inquiry. They also contributed significantly to the whole process of feminist 're-vision' which has led to a radical revaluation of the critical givens of a predominantly male liter-ary establishment, interrogating the construction and validity of the literary canon and rejecting qualities such as objectivity, unity and rationality as the *sine qua non* of literary merit and importance.

Much early feminist criticism was positively hostile to theory, regarding it as 'masculine' in its schematising and pseudo-scientism. This work was informed more by a politics 'of *asking women's questions*' than by specific engagement with particular critical theories.[46] Such criticism was frequently – indeed, often quite insistently – personal, and tended to quarry the work for its relevance to feminist concerns. So, for example, in '*Jane Eyre*: Woman's estate', Maurianne Adams describes the experience of rereading *Jane Eyre* as an adult as 'unnerving to say the least', and finds that it leads her in-evitably to 'feminist issues, by which I mean the status and economics of female dependence in marriage, the limited options available to Jane as an outlet for her education and energies, her need to love and be loved, to be of service and to be needed'.[47] Similarly, in '*Jane Eyre*: The temptations of a motherless woman', Adrienne Rich claims that in rereading Brontë's novel through the years she has derived 'nourishment I needed then and still need today', and she sees in Jane's journey a succession of triumphs over 'certain traditional female temptations'.[48]

Even with the advance in theoretical sophistication provided by critics such as Gilbert and Gubar, much feminist criticism still demonstrated the persistence of certain beliefs which linked it with the traditional assumptions it sought to oppose. So, for example, as a number of critiques have pointed out, Gilbert and Gubar's work is typical of much 'first-wave' feminist criticism in the totalising aspect of both its reading of women's literature as inevitably 'revisionary and revolutionary' and its representation of patriarchal ideology as non-contradictory and monolithically oppressive. Failing to account for the seemingly miraculous immunity that allows women to write subversively, Gilbert and Gubar accept the woman writer as the authoritative source or 'transcendental signified' of the text. Toril Moi sees this tenacity of traditional theoretical assumptions as the main problem with what she calls 'Anglo-American' feminist criticism, because it leads to a radical contradiction between 'feminist politics and patriarchal aesthetics'.[49]

Since Moi levelled that criticism, however, feminist literary studies have continued to develop, demonstrating not only an increasing theoretical sophistication but a growing political maturity. Just as the women's movement began with the celebration of 'sisterhood' and 'solidarity', based on a sense of being able to speak unproblematically of 'woman' and 'women's experience', and has subsequently been forced to recognise the distortion and oppression of such hegemonic practice for Third World, coloured, working-class and lesbian women, so feminist criticism has become more self-reflexive and self-critical, and has been compelled to confront its own occlusions. Gayatri Spivak, for example, in her essay 'Three women's texts and a critique of imperialism' (1985), has criticised a tendency in feminist criticism 'to reproduce the axioms of imperialism', and offered a telling critique of *Jane Eyre*, not in an effort to impugn Brontë's standing with feminists, but 'to situate feminist individualism in its historical determination rather than simply to canonize it as feminism as such'.[50] Her analysis centres on the figure of the half-caste Bertha Mason, whose function, Spivak claims, is 'to render indeterminate the boundary between human and animal and thereby weaken her entitlement under the spirit, if not the letter, of the Law'.[51] Similarly, Penny Boumelha argues that one of the central problems of Brontë's novel, and of certain feminist readings of it, lies with 'the apparently blithe predication of the liberty and happiness of a few upon the confinement and suffering of the many'. She points to the class- and race-blindness of many feminist readings of the novel, suggesting that the focus on Jane's individualist narrative obscures the stories of 'those other women', Bessie, Grace Poole and Bertha Mason. Accordingly, she urges contemporary feminist criticism not to reproduce 'the silences and occlusions of nineteenth-century English culture in allowing the white, middle-class woman to stand as its own "paradigmatic woman"'.[52]

These challenges to the ideological awareness of feminist criticism have been accompanied by the challenge of new theoretical perspectives. They have not invalidated those pioneering 'heroic' readings of the text offered by critics such as Adrienne Rich and Maurianne Adams, but they have recognised the need for feminist criticism to find a way to retain that sense of the 'relevance' of the reading and the 'worldliness' of the text, while at the same time rigorously scrutinising its bases. The terms of the discussion have become much more com- plex and shifting – post-structuralism has problematised any assumption of a direct and simple relationship between author, text and reader, discourse theory has challenged any claim to an objective knowledge of history, and deconstruction and psychoanalysis have disrupted a sense of fixed meaning, interrogating both the seeming integrity of the realist text and the unity of its subject.

Feminist critics have shown every sign of rising to the challenge through the strategic use of a range of theoretical tools. Patricia Yaeger, in 'Honey-mad women: Charlotte Brontë's bilingual heroines', for example, provides a symptomatic reading of *Jane Eyre*'s 'subversive multi-voicedness', arguing that Brontë's use of a second language 'serves an emancipatory function in Brontë's texts, enacting a moment in which the novel's primary language is put into process, a moment of process, a moment of possible transformation when the writer forces her speech to break out of old representations of the feminine and to posit something new'.[53] Yaeger suggests that the 'other' or foreign language can be used to signalise what is repressed, as though fantastically escaping the logocentrism of the Symbolic Order. She argues that when representations of a foreign language system appear in Brontë's novels, 'we find an image not of the word as limit – something feminist theory has taught us to expect – but the word as victor, as harbinger of an abnormal way of thinking that is capable, in its strangeness, of bringing the heroine into dialogue with something new'.[54] So, for example, Yaeger suggests that Brontë creates a 'utopian moment' when, in the schoolroom at Lowood, 'the derogatory word [slattern] is burned and replaced by the verb "Etre" – evoking sonority in Jane's own name, revealing "Eyre" as a cognate for the verb "to be" '.[55] In a similar reading of the 'politics of style', Margaret Homans, in *Bearing the Word: Language and female experience in nineteenth-century women's writing*, investigates *Jane Eyre* at the level of both 'theme and literary practice' as an example of 'women's revisions of the cultural myth of women's place in language', arguing that Brontë and various nineteenth-century women authors 'are writing and practicing myths of daughters' relations to symbolic language, working out through their writing the conflicts between being a daughter and being a writer'.[56] Mary Poovey, too, draws on a range of theoretical perspectives to demonstrate the value of new historicist practice for feminists in *Uneven Developments* by examining the 'ideology of gender' in mid-Victorian England in a variety of discursive fields, including its literary manifestation in *Jane Eyre*. In all, feminist criticism, with its plurality, adaptability and political commitment, continues to offer the most persuasive and enlightening readings of Charlotte Brontë's work.

II

Jane Eyre
A Reading of the Text

1

Motherhood

In her pioneering essay on *Jane Eyre*, Adrienne Rich established and celebrated the importance of a maternal presence in the novel, arguing that 'Jane Eyre, motherless and economically powerless, undergoes certain traditional female temptations, and finds that each temptation presents itself along with an alternative – the image of a nurturing or principled or spirited woman on whom she can model herself, or to whom she can look for support.'[1] Rich also sees the workings of a more generalised 'matriarchal aspect' in the interventions of the natural world, which are imaged in distinctly maternal terms. It is a persuasive reading, drawing attention to the succession of mother figures who populate Jane's pilgrimage and act as 'mediators for her along the way'.[2]

Bessie is the first such figure, providing Jane with her only source of affection and support in the emotional desolation of Gateshead. Though Bessie is an unreliable ally, given to vagaries of temper and inclined to co-option in the prevailing harsh judgments of Jane, she does offer Jane some semblance of desperately needed physical and emotional nurturance, frequently smuggling 'a bun or a cheese-cake'[3] from the kitchen and diverting the ostracised Jane with songs, stories and 'now and then a word of unwonted kindness' (20). In this way she anticipates the intervention of a number of supportive mother figures throughout the novel.

At Lowood the idealised Miss Temple, 'gentle, concerned' and 'full of goodness', provides Jane with 'continual solace;

she had stood me in the stead of mother, governess, and, latterly, companion' (84). She protects Jane to the best of her ability from the injustice and meanness of Lowood's patriarch, Mr Brocklehurst. She is also instrumental in the education which is to provide a means of economic self-sufficiency for Jane. Similarly, Helen Burns offers Jane intellectual companionship, moral guidance and a constancy of affection: 'at all times and under all circumstances, [Helen] evinced for me a quiet and faithful friendship' (79). Helen also provides Jane with physical intimacy to assuage her deprivation, beginning with the comfort she offers after Brocklehurst's humiliating denunciation of Jane: 'Resting my head on Helen's shoulder, I put my arms around her waist; she drew me to her, and we reposed in silence' (70), and concluding with their tender embrace on Helen's deathbed: 'And I clasped my arms closer round Helen: she seemed dearer to me than ever; I felt as if I could not let her go; I lay with my face hidden on her neck' (83).

In the next episode of Jane's life she is welcomed with warmth and kindness to Thornfield Hall by the good-spirited Mrs Fairfax. Subsequently, at Moor House, she is sheltered from the freezing elements, and from St John's chilling 'evangelical charity', by the Rivers sisters, whose names, Diana and Mary, associate them with childbirth and motherhood in pagan and Christian mythology. Like Miss Temple before her, Diana feeds Jane, supports her in her resistance to St John's demands, and plays 'the part of instructress': 'I was fain to sit on a stool at Diana's feet, to rest my head on her knee . . . I liked to learn of her' (355).

As Adrienne Rich has argued, Jane is also protected throughout the novel by a powerful maternal force embodied in the natural world, which finds particular focus in the moon. So, for example, in her flight from Thornfield she is nourished by the 'universal mother': 'Nature seemed to me benign and good: I thought she loved me, outcast as I was; and I, who from man could anticipate only mistrust, rejection, insult, clung to her with filial fondness. Tonight, at least, I would be her guest

– as I was her child: my mother would lodge me without money and without price' (328). This natural maternal supervision is as direct as any offered by Jane's earthly surrogates – first when the moon admonishes Jane to leave Rochester:

> It spoke, to my spirit: immeasurably distant was the tone, yet so near, it whispered in my heart –
> 'My daughter, flee temptation!'
> 'Mother, I will.' (324)

– and again when she prays for guidance in the face of St John's coercive marriage proposal and mysteriously hears Rochester's desperate entreaty: 'it is the work of nature. She was roused, and did – no miracle – but her best' (425).

In all, then, it does seem valid to argue in keeping with Rich, and as I have elsewhere, that *Jane Eyre* 'explores a craving within the heroine which is met by a nourishing, supportive maternal capacity in a series of female figures who populate her pilgrimage and, more broadly, in a prevailing female presence in the natural world'.[4]

What such an argument fails to take into account, however, is the deep ambivalence evident in the novel towards mothers and mothering. Indeed, part of Jane's craving for maternal affection, it should be recognised, stems precisely from the startling failure of her guardian and original mother figure, Mrs Reed, to provide nurture. So, the corollary of these benevolent mother figures is the figure of the malevolent maternal character. In setting up this division Brontë draws on an archetypal literary dichotomy – one which is most familiar, perhaps, in its folk-tale version of the fairy godmother and the wicked stepmother or witch.

One way of understanding the attraction to this division more generally is to see it as stemming from a universal and fundamental ambivalence towards the mother figure which has been extensively documented in imaginative and scientific literature alike. At base this ambivalence is an expression of essentially conflicting desires on the one hand for nurturance and on the other for autonomy, a wish at once for dependence upon, and independence from, the mother. In this scheme of things the child is impelled to define herself simultaneously with, and against, the mother – the first position promises security and comfort, yet threatens immersion and self-erasure; while the second promises separateness and self-identity, but threatens loneliness and painful loss. Nancy Chodorow and Susan Contratto have argued that one consequence of this ambivalence is the impulse both to blame and to idealise the mother, which has become part of our cultural ideology. This idealisation and blaming are, they argue, 'two sides of the same belief in the all-powerful mother'.[5] Similarly, Elizabeth Grosz, in her discussion of the French feminist theorist Luce Irigaray, points to the seeming inevitability of this dichotomy under patriarchy:

> As mother, her material and economic possibilities are severely limited. Cut off from social and sexual recognition, she becomes either the mother who gives *too much* of herself (the suffocating mother, represented in Woody Allen's film *Interiors*); or the mother who gives *too little* (the selfish mother, represented in Ingmar Bergman's *Autumn Sonata*). These represent the two extremes of maternity in a culture which refuses to acknowledge the woman who is (and is more than) the mother.[6]

The recourse to fairy godmothers and wicked stepmothers in literature allows for a separation of these competing and irreconcilable desires – an artificial resolution of a painful confusion of feeling is achieved by ascribing single characteristics to separate figures. So, for example, in *Jane Eyre* one 'mother', Mrs Reed, features as an agent of oppression who elicits anger and hatred; while another, Miss Temple, operates as an ally against oppression who inspires love and devotion. Similar patterns are evident, too, in Brontë's second novel, *Shirley*, in the split between Hortense and Mrs Pryor, and in her final work, *Villette*, in the division between Madame Beck and Mrs Bretton.

As I have suggested, Brontë is not unusual in employing this strategy of division in dealing with motherhood. It is the stuff of archetypal childhood fantasies – as much the plight of Snow

White and Cinderella as of Jane Eyre and Lucy Snowe. However, I think there are good reasons to suggest that such splitting of the maternal subject is more relevant to women authors and their female characters than to their male counterparts. First, from a psychoanalytic perspective the threat of engulfment or immersion is more potent for the girl child, whose gender identification with the mother compounds the difficulties of separation. Thus, Nancy Chodorow explains the tenacity of the girl child's pre-Oedipal attachment:

> All children must free themselves from their mother's omnipotence and gain a sense of completeness. Insofar as a boy achieves this liberation, he does so through his masculinity and possession of a penis. A boy's mother, living in a male-dominant society, and in a family where her husband is not around as much as her son, cathects him heterosexually precisely on account of his maleness. (This also has costs for the boy.) His penis and masculinity both compensate the boy for his early narcissistic injuries and symbolize his independence and separateness from his mother.
>
> A girl's experience is likely to be different on two counts. A daughter does not have something different and desirable with which to oppose maternal omnipotence, as does a son. Equally important, however, is that 'the mother does not cathect her daughter in the same way that she cathects her son' in the first place: She does not cathect her as a sexual other, but as part of a narcissistically defined self.[7]

Secondly, from a sociohistorical perspective, the forms of rebellion which might facilitate adequate separation from the mother – are and, more particularly, have been – culturally less available to women. Whereas literature – and life – offer heroic models of male rivalry, where self-identification is achieved through surpassing the father, the expressions of aggression and sexuality which might make this possible for the woman have been largely taboo. One solution, then, has been to create wicked stepmothers who warrant the hostility they both attract and inspire.[8]

For Charlotte Brontë in *Jane Eyre* the division of her maternal figures into good and bad surrogates allowed both the creation of some fantasies and the exposure of others. In opening the novel with the 'wicked' Mrs Reed, for example, Brontë allowed her heroine a triumphant moment of assertion:

> 'I'm glad you are no relative of mine: I will never call you aunt again as long as I live. I will never come to see you when I am grown up; and if any one asks me how I liked you, and how you treated me, I will say the very thought of you makes me sick, and that you treated me with miserable cruelty.' (37)

It is a child's fantasy of rage, all the more satisfying because it is fully warranted by Mrs Reed's simple – and simplified – malevolence. More importantly, the novel's early chapters, so coloured by Mrs Reed's cruelty and injustice, enable Brontë to explore the negative aspects of the maternal without transgressing the ideal, seeing in the substitute mother what might be too painful to face in the natural mother. The opening page, for example, presents the spectre of the socialising force of the mother in her role as the agent, if not the origin, of authority. Maternal affection is exposed as contingent upon conformity and acquiescence:

> Me, she had dispensed from joining the group; saying, 'She regretted to be under the necessity of keeping me at a distance; but that until she heard from Bessie, and could discover by her own observation that I was endeavouring in good earnest to acquire a more sociable and child-like disposition, a more attractive and sprightly manner, – something lighter, franker, more natural as it were – she really must exclude me from the privileges intended only for contented, happy little children.' (7)

Similarly, when Mrs Reed acts as Jane's jailor in the red-room, she offers the child liberation 'only on condition of perfect submission and stillness' (18).

Jane's misery at Gateshead constitutes a child's nightmare of lack of control, and of dependence devoid of affection. She claims that she was 'never . . . happy' in Mrs Reed's presence, and that 'however carefully I obeyed, however strenuously I strove to please her, my efforts were still repulsed . . .' (34). Not surprisingly, in the midst of her oppression, when the servant Bessie offers to fetch her a book, Jane requests *Gulliver's Travels*, a fantasy of power reversal akin to her momentary victory when she stands 'winner of the field' against Mrs Reed. The negativity of the maternal finds a primary focus in the horror of the red-room, in some respects a womb-like space yet a chill and deadly enclosure, 'remote from the nursery and kitchens' (14) – removed, that is, from nurturing and nutriment.

Significantly, against this maternal coldness Brontë holds up a succession of images of masculine comfort and support. In her internment in the red-room Jane imagines 'that if Mr. Reed had been alive he would have treated me kindly' (16). Her conjecture is sound since her uncle has, in fact, tended the infant Jane: 'Reed pitied it; and he used to nurse it and notice it as if it had been his own' (234); in striking contrast to Mrs Reed's unmaternal abhorrence: 'I hated it the first time I set my eyes on it – a sickly, whining, pining thing!' (234). Similarly, when Jane regains consciousness in the nursery after her terrified collapse in the red-room, she becomes aware 'that someone was handling me; lifting me up and supporting me in a sitting posture: and that more tenderly than I had ever been raised or upheld before' (18). This unsurpassed tenderness, we discover, is meted out by Mr Lloyd, the apothecary. And finally Bessie's song, which moves Jane to tears, offers the ultimate image of paternal protection:

> Still will my Father, with promise and blessing,
> Take to his bosom the poor orphan child. (22)

These images might be seen as prefiguring both Jane's later choices, which turn her 'back to patriarchal determinations of kinship and inheritance',[9] and the novel's ending, which fantastically reverses Jane's predicament, transforming the orphan, dependent and unloved, into the wife, depended upon and adored.

Even leaving aside the ambivalence evident in the splitting of the mother figures in the novel, the issue of maternity in *Jane Eyre* is more complex than any simple celebration of the inspiring and supportive surrogates will allow, because the dichotomies of 'good' and 'bad' themselves will not hold.

When examined more closely, the love and nurturance of the 'good' mothers threaten to damage, while the hostility and neglect of the 'bad' mothers promise to liberate.

In the opening pages of the novel, Mrs Reed functions not only as the type of the wicked stepmother for Jane but also as the parody of the smothering attendant mother, overfeeding and overindulging her son John to the detriment of his health, character and intellect:

> He gorged himself habitually at table, which made him bilious, and gave him a dim and bleared eye and flabby cheeks. He ought now to have been at school; but his mama had taken him home for a month or two, 'on account of his delicate health.' Mr. Miles, the master, affirmed that he would do very well if he had fewer cakes and sweetmeats sent from home; but the mother's heart turned from an opinion so harsh and inclined rather to the more refined idea that John's sallowness was owing to over-application and, perhaps, to pining after home. (10)

The ministrations of Jane's maternal surrogates are never so grotesque, but the novel does betray a consistent awareness, even anxiety, about the anaesthetising quality of the maternal attention Jane receives. Thus, for example, she observes a calmness about Miss Temple, who 'always had something of serenity in her air, of state in her mien, of refined propriety in her language, which precluded deviation into the ardent, the excited, the eager' (73). Helen Burns, similarly, imparts 'tranquillity' (70) to Jane. In the face of their combined influence, Miss Temple admonishing that Jane should 'exaggerate nothing' and Helen warning against 'the indulgence of resentment' (71), Jane gives an account of her life which is 'most moderate . . . restrained and simplified' (71). Ironically, though, the power and impact of Brontë's novel have always been due to the very opposite qualities – that is, to the impassioned nature of Jane's narrative, to its status as an 'autobiography' that vehemently insists: 'Nobody knows how many rebellions besides political rebellions ferment in the masses of life which people earth. Women are supposed to be very calm generally: but women feel just as men feel' (110).

   This distortion of Jane's tale in its brief rendition to Miss Temple, which is symptomatic of the distortion of personality Jane suffers at Lowood, threatens to subvert her whole enterprise of recollection. Under the tranquillising influence of her mentors, Jane is in danger of having no story to tell:

> Hitherto I have recorded in detail the events of my insignificant existence: to the first ten years of my life, I have given almost as many chapters. But this is not to be regular autobiography: I am only bound to invoke memory where I know her responses will possess some degree of interest; therefore I now pass a space of eight years almost in silence: a few lines only are necessary to keep up the links of connection. (83)

This ellipsis, or silence, amounts in one sense to a loss or effacement of the self, a lapse in the self-identifying process, since in the terms of the narrative, the self exists only through the story – or, as Natalie Sarraute writes in her autobiographical novel *Childhood*, 'I am nothing other than what I have written'.[10] This loss is underscored by the vagueness and lack of definition with which the narrator alludes to her existence during the greater part of her time at Lowood. Describing her life during those eight years as 'uniform', Jane can offer only negatives to characterise her experience: '[it was] not unhappy, because it was not inactive' (84). Similarly, whereas in other parts of the novel Jane's imagination is marked by a sharpness of perception, her recollection at this point appears to lack any surety of grasp, with its emphasis on seeming:

> I had imbibed from her something of her nature and much of her habits: more harmonious thoughts, what *seemed* better regulated feelings had become the inmates of my mind. I had given in allegiance to duty and order; I was quiet; I *believed* I was content: to the eyes of others, *usually* even to my own, I *appeared* a disciplined and subdued character. (85; emphasis added)

   At Lowood Jane has occupied a world of 'duty and order', 'rules and systems' (83) as an 'inmate of its walls' (84). She has done so with the encouragement of Helen Burns and Miss Temple, who have inculcated in her the values of endurance and obedience. As I have suggested elsewhere, both women offer Jane important examples of alternative behaviour.[11] Helen's 'doctrine of endurance' (56) provides an important counter to Jane's earlier explosive rebellion, which even the child Jane recognises is ultimately as destructive as it is immediately satisfying: 'Something of vengeance I had tasted for the first time; as aromatic wine it seemed on swallowing, warm and racy: its after-flavour, metallic and corroding, gave me a sensation as if I had been poisoned' (38). Furthermore, Helen's stoicism furnishes a useful check to Jane's dangerously slavish desire for love. When Jane rashly declares:

> 'if others don't love me, I would rather die than live – I cannot bear to be solitary and hated, Helen. Look here; to gain some real affection from you, or Miss Temple, or any other whom I truly love, I would willingly submit to have the bone of my arm broken, or to let a bull toss me, or to stand behind a kicking horse and let it dash its hoofs at my chest –'(70)

Helen stems this masochistic litany with a timely warning: 'Hush, Jane! you think too much of the love of human beings' (70). More importantly, she insists that Jane recognise the primacy of the individual conscience, and that she cease to look to external authority for the validation she must find within: 'If all the world hated you, and believed you wicked, while your own conscience approved you, and absolved you from guilt, you would not be without friends' (70).

None the less, Helen's lessons of endurance have their negative aspect. Her espousal of justice and satisfaction in the hereafter – 'God waits only the separation of spirit from flesh to crown us with a full reward. Why, then, should we ever sink overwhelmed with distress, when life is so soon over, and death is so certain an entrance to happiness: to glory?' (70) – offers a standard repressive strategy, characteristically employed in the interests of conservatism to defer or diffuse resistance to present injustice. Helen's own life – and, more importantly, her death – are emblematic of the self-erasure consequent upon such a relentless and unmitigated attachment to a 'doctrine of endurance' (56).

Miss Temple's example to Jane is similarly ambiguous. Certainly her demonstration of a temperate and principled resistance to injustice provides a further counterbalance to Jane's excessive and destructive tantrums at Gateshead. However, while Miss Temple does ameliorate the abuses of the system at Lowood, dispensing food and publicly repudiating Brocklehurst's unjust charges against Jane, she none the less still operates very much within it. Admittedly, the power she enjoys as directress of the institution is undercut by the restrictions she suffers in being answerable to Brocklehurst as an employee. Yet even when her authority is potentially paramount – as when Mrs Harden, the housekeeper, refuses to supply the extra toast she has requested – she is surprisingly acquiescent: ' "Oh, very well!" returned Miss Temple; "we must make do, Barbara, I suppose" ' (73). More disturbing, in her efforts to function within the system, Miss Temple is in danger of taking on the qualities she resists. So, while Jane describes Brocklehurst as a 'rigid', 'black column' (62), she notes similarly that Miss Temple stands before him, 'her face, naturally pale as marble, appeared to be assuming also the coldness and fixity of that material: especially her mouth closed as if it would have required a sculptor's chisel to open it, and her brow settled gradually into petrified severity' (64).

Jane does not wake herself from her torpor at Lowood; rather, she is rudely awoken. Only with Miss Temple's marriage and departure does Jane lose her 'reason for tranquillity' (85). The artificial nature of the 'Lowood constraint' (140), which has become such a part of her demeanour, is evident in the rapidity with which her 'borrowed' disposition gives way in its 'natural element' to 'old emotions': 'From the day she left I was no longer the same' (85).

Jane has paid a high price for 'maternal' approval, adopting the conformity or mimicry of the 'good' daughter playing a part to the 'good' mother. It is not until she is deprived of the 'maternal' presence that she begins to manifest once more the 'courage to go forth' (85), the quality we perhaps most associate with her female heroism. No longer content to be an 'inmate', Jane moves to the window and surveys with longing the remotest limits of the horizon: 'all within their boundary of rock and heath seemed prison-ground, exile limits' (85).

The stultifying atmosphere of Lowood is repeated at Thornfield – at least for as long as the house is presided over by the motherly Mrs Fairfax:

> I did not like re-entering Thornfield. To pass its threshold was to return to stagnation: to cross the silent hall, to ascend the darksome staircase, to seek my own lonely little room, and then to meet tranquil Mrs. Fairfax, and spend the long winter evening with her and her only, was to quell wholly the faint excitement wakened by my walk, – to slip again over my faculties the viewless fetters of an uniform and too still existence. (117)

The association of this stasis with the female is made even more explicit when Rochester's advent is represented as transformational and enlivening: 'I discerned in the course of the morning that Thornfield Hall was a changed place . . . a rill from the outer world was flowing through it; it had a master: for my part, I liked it better' (119).

At Moor-House Jane repeats the pattern of self-submersion established at Lowood, stalling her journey in her cousins' secluded home at Marsh End. Indeed, before Jane's exodus from Thornfield the forward momentum of her quest has not only been stalled but actually reversed in her return to Gateshead to visit the dying Mrs Reed. The regressive nature of that journey is first made clear in Jane's interaction with Bessie. She takes pleasure, for example, in submitting to Bessie's ministrations 'just as passively as I used to let her undress me when a child' (229), and in Bessie's providing refreshments 'absolutely as she used to accommodate me with some privately purloined dainty on a nursery chair' (229). Despite her well-founded conviction that Mrs Reed had 'ever hated me' (242) and that it was in her aunt's nature 'to wound me cruelly' (34), Jane has returned to Gateshead with 'an aching heart' (230) and with a 'strong yearning' to 'be reconciled' (232). Of course, she finds Mrs Reed implacable in her hostility, 'unchanged, and unchangeable' (233), but the incident confirms the potentially regressive nature of the yearning for maternal love and approval.

Jane's cousin Diana exhorts her to 'be obedient' (349), and at Moor-House Jane is once more overwhelmed by an attractive and intelligent female figure who offers her nurture and ministration. Accordingly, she finds that she takes 'pleasure in yielding to an authority' (348) like Diana's, and a certain stasis overtakes her again. In a curious echo of the atrophy suggested by images of 'petrified severity' associated with Miss Temple, Diana's name is shortened to 'Die' in the discussion of their uncle's death, a context which makes the obvious association with morbidity quite clear. In her clinging 'tenaciously to the ties of flesh' (395) Jane forswears any determination to 'go forth': 'I will live at Moor-House . . . I will attach myself for life to Diana and Mary' (391). Thus, ironically, the contentment she could not muster to earn Mrs Reed's approval at the beginning of the novel, she determinedly embraces at Moor-House: ' "St. John," I said, "I think you are almost wicked to talk so. I am disposed to be as content as a queen, and you try to stir me up to restlessness!" ' (395).

Repeatedly, then, whereas the maternal offers comfort and tranquillity in the novel, within those very terms it also threatens stagnation and immersion. Furthermore, in contrast to the stasis associated with Jane's positive mother figures, her 'bad' mothers impel her forward in her journey. Mrs Reed literally expels Jane from the home and out into the 'expanse' of the 'real world' that she as heroine finds so challenging: 'Thus was I severed from Bessie and Gateshead: thus whirled away to unknown, and, as I then deemed, remote and mysterious regions' (42). Similarly, while Bertha Mason's visit to Jane's bedroom on the eve of her marriage to Rochester may be seen in Rochester's terms as 'malignant' (287), it is also possible to see Bertha's intervention as comparable with the natural omens that warn Jane against the union and urge her to leave Thornfield. It is, after all, the expensive wedding veil bought by Rochester, not Jane herself, that Bertha attacks.

What we find, then, is a shifting and ambiguous quality in

the dichotomy between 'good' and 'bad' mothers in the novel, and this is further complicated by the fact that Jane's 'good' mother figures are not mothers at all. Of course, biological maternity is not a necessary precondition for such surrogacy; nevertheless there is a curious insistence on the virginal quality of Jane's 'mothers'. Bessie, for example, is a mere girl, not much older than Jane herself, when she 'mothers' the outcast in the Reed family, and Helen Burns is similarly childlike. Maria Temple, whose purity is suggested in her name, disappears from Jane's life at the exact moment when she forfeits her virginal status in marriage. Accordingly, while there has never been any suggestion of courtship before the wedding, at the first mention of Miss Temple's husband, Jane also notes that her mentor 'consequently was lost to me' (84). Similarly, Diana's and Mary's names exemplify their chaste existence. Whereas both names, as suggested, are linked with maternity, they are equally associated with virginity – Diana (or Artemis) as the pagan Virgin Huntress, and Mary as the Christian Virgin Mother. In this refusal to see maternity linked with sexuality, to see the mother as woman, Brontë reflects a perspective deeply entrenched in the cultural ideology of patriarchy which will be examined in further detail in the next chapter. The polarisation is even clearer when one recognises that against this array of virginal figures the two women who are defined as sexual beings – Mrs Reed with her three young children and Bertha Mason with her licentious appetite – are both seen as monstrous. The womb-like spaces most associated with each of them, the red-room and the attic respectively, are chambers of mystery and horror, and in the case of Bertha her monstrousness is linked specifically to the maternal line. So, she is the 'true daughter of an infamous mother' (310), while her younger brother, as 'a complete dumb idiot' (310), enjoys a significantly more benign inheritance.

Given a deep ambivalence to maternity, then, reflected variously in the polarisation of good and bad mothers, and complicated by the shifting and uncertain nature of those qualities, it is not surprising that Charlotte Brontë is drawn in some degree to a notion of motherlessness. It would be overly simple to try to explain away the orphan status of all Brontë's heroines by reference to her own biography.[12] Certainly, Charlotte lost her mother when she was only 5 years old, and was 'made motherless' a second time when her eldest sister Maria died four years later.[13] However, such a biographical explanation cannot account for the fact that the motherlessness of Brontë's heroines links them with a wide range of other orphaned nineteenth-century heroines, all of whom suffer from what Elizabeth Barrett Browning, in her epic of the motherless Aurora Leigh, called a 'mother-want'. Indeed, Florence Nightingale went so far as to claim this phenomenon as one of the principal virtues of the mid-nineteenth-century novel: 'the secret charm of every romance', she wrote, 'is that the heroine has *generally* no family ties (almost *invariably* no mother)'.[14]

This general inclination, particularly on the part of women writers, to create motherless heroines can be explained in two ways. In the first place, the absence of the mother can obviate the guilt of separation for the heroine; in the second, it can liberate the heroine into heroic self-sufficiency. Various theorists of childhood have underlined the need for the child to formulate and assert their identity by separation from the parent, and particularly the mother. So, for example, Nancy Chodorow argues: 'All children must free themselves from their mother's omnipotence and gain a sense of completeness'.[15] Similarly, Elizabeth Grosz, in discussing Luce Irigaray's *Et l'une ne bouge pas sans l'autre*, notes Irigaray's description of 'a suffocating maternal bond which it must sooner or later attempt to flee in order to have any identity'.[16] As we have seen, that separation from the mother is particularly difficult for girls for both psychological and sociohistorical reasons. We have seen that one solution to this ambivalence towards the mother is imaginatively to separate conflicting desires and emotions into good and bad mother figures, allowing the latter to be rejected, and hence separated from, with impunity. However, as noted, even 'good' mother figures can smother or immerse, albeit less threateningly than the natural mother in the Oedipal configuration. Another solution to this daughterly dilemma is to banish the mother, liberating the heroine by maternal absence. So, for example, on the occasion of Jane's departure from Gateshead, it is not Mrs Reed's cruelty but her absence that is stressed:

> As we passed Mrs. Reed's bed-room, she said, 'Will you go in and bid Missis good-bye?'
> 'No, Bessie: she came to my crib last night when you were gone down to supper, and said I need not disturb her in the morning, or my cousins either.' (41)

Without attachment, Jane is liberated to respond unconventionally to the rift, as she embraces rather than regrets her separateness: 'Probably, if I had left a good home and kind parents, this would have been the hour when I should most keenly have regretted the separation . . . as it was I derived from both a strange excitement, and reckless and feverish, I wished the wind to howl more wildly, the gloom to deepen to darkness, and the confusion to rise to clamour' (55).

In one sense, then, Jane's motherlessness, far from being a source of deprivation, is a source of liberation and an essential factor in her heroic quest. Put simply: if Jane could go home to mother after the shocking discovery of Rochester's bigamous intent, *Jane Eyre* would be a very different – and considerably shorter – novel. In fact, the novel suggests a direct relation between deprivation and self-sufficiency. The young girl who lavishes affection on her doll 'in the dearth of worthier objects of affection' (28) is also the child who takes care of herself – 'when the embers sank to dull red, I undressed hastily, tugging at knots and strings as I best might' (28) – in contrast to her pampered cousins, who are daily costumed and coiffed like dolls: 'dressed out in their muslin frocks and scarlet sashes, with hair elaborately ringletted' (28). Consequently, Jane's claim later in life – '*I* care for myself' (321) – has resonance in more than one sense. In all, her nature as 'a little roving, solitary thing' (39), which forms the basis of her questing, autonomous, heroic self, is inextricably linked with her outcast status as an orphan.

Through the absence of a mother, Jane, like many other heroines, escapes the restrictive legacy that the mother, as the principal agent of socialisation, bequeaths to the daughter:

> 'Guilt and self-blame', 'shame and embarrassment', entrapment and helplessness: these constitute, at least in part, the heritage passed between mothers and daughters in a recurrent cyclical process which can result in emotional impoverishment, paralysis and death.[17]

We have seen the spectre of Mrs Reed's socialising demands and the effect of stultification which comes with Jane's acquiescence in the desire for maternal approval, but in both cases the influence is more sporadic and Jane is less enmeshed than one might expect were she dealing with a biological mother, where bonds of nurture and sameness run deeper. Similarly, the maternal force that Brontë locates in nature proves infinitely more amenable and tractable in Jane's heroic script than any biological mother figure could plausibly be. Not only does her 'universal mother' guide her away from Rochester in the first instance, but she intervenes to send her back to him, thus validating Jane's sexual choice of Rochester over St John in a way that no conceivable nineteenth-century maternal character could.

According to the psychoanalyst D. W. Winnicott, the nursing mother's face provides a mirror which offers the daughter a place to confirm her identity, but as Ellen Rosenman points out, 'insofar as it already presumes an approved image, it is also coercive and threatens the daughter's sense of self, urging her into mere imitation'.[18] It is perhaps emblematic, then, that when Jane is sent to the red-room, deemed a deceitful and uncontrollable ingrate by Mrs Reed, she fails to recognise her own image in the mirror, as though as outcast and orphan she is spared the internalisation of the 'mother's' coercive reflection. In the end it may well be that the self-actualising daughter – the author, and the heroine of the nineteenth-century novel – has needed to kill the mother-in-the-house as much as Virginia Woolf needed to kill the oppressive angel-in-the-house.[19]

Jane's liberation from the mother figure is matched in a way by her liberation from motherhood. Although she does in the end bear Rochester a son, there is much in the novel to suggest the heroine's unconscious rejection of the role of mother. In a dream on the eve of her wedding, for example, Jane sees herself 'burdened with the charge of a little child' (284). Despite the child's helplessness – 'a very small creature, too young and feeble to walk, and which shivered in my cold arms, and wailed piteously in my ear' (284) – her attention is wholly taken up by her efforts to reach Rochester on the road ahead. That overwhelming desire is represented as being directly at odds with the nursing of the child: 'I strained every nerve to overtake you and made effort on effort to utter your name and entreat you to stop – but my movements were fettered' (284). In a subsequent dream Jane is once more nightmarishly burdened with the small child: 'I might not lay it down anywhere, however tired were my arms – however much its weight impeded my progress' (285). This time, in her 'frantic' haste to catch sight of Rochester, the child becomes a casualty of her desire: 'I bent forward to take a last look; the wall crumbled; I was shaken; the child rolled from my knee' (285). An unconscious negativity towards motherhood is evident, too, in Jane's use of metaphor. So, for example, when she contemplates the prospect of Rochester marrying Blanche Ingram and leaving her, she suppresses the painful thought, saying: 'I strangled a new-born agony – a deformed thing which I could not persuade myself to own and rear' (246).

Jane's choice in the dream of her lover ahead of her infant charge is repeated in reality the next day when she takes her leave of Adèle:

> I remember Adèle clung to me as I left her: I remember I kissed her as I loosened her little hands from my neck; and I cried over her with strange emotion, and quitted her because I feared my sobs would break her still sound repose. She seemed the emblem of my past life; and he, I was now to array myself to meet, the dread, but adored, type of my unknown future day. (289)

Even more revealingly, Jane abandons Adèle a second time. When Jane is finally settled with Rochester at Ferndean, she sends for Adèle to come home from boarding school with the intention of becoming 'her governess once more' (455). Despite clear signs of deprivation – 'She looked pale and thin: she said she was not happy' (455) – and despite Adèle's 'frantic joy' at the reunion, the priorities of the dream are quickly reasserted. Jane finds the plan to keep Adèle at home impracticable – 'my time and cares were now required by another – my husband needed them all' (455) – and she sends her away to school once more. Ironically, if Adèle's plight is reminiscent of the young Jane at Gateshead, Jane's action is reminiscent of Mrs Reed's.

In striking contrast to the passion of much of Jane's language, her commentary on Adèle is uncharacteristically remote. She herself comments on the unusually 'cool language' with which she speaks of her charge, and significantly, that detachment becomes even more pronounced in relation to her own child. In what almost amounts to a total effacement from the text, Jane refers to her son only twice – as 'his first-born' and 'the boy' (457).

One way of understanding Jane's refusal of the role of mother in her dreams and in her actions is to see it simply as a choice in favour of the role of wife – that is, a choice for a sexual identity ahead of a maternal one in the terms of the polarity already discussed. It seems, however, that there is more at stake. Elizabeth Grosz argues:

> Maternity under patriarchy curtails the mother's ability to act as a woman. It also implies an 'exile' for the daughter, for she is cut off from access to the woman-mother; and thus from her own potential as a woman. She has no *woman* with whom to identify. She can take on the socially validated place as a mother herself only by replacing her mother, by 'killing' her: 'Women are torn from their first desires, their sexuality. And they never find a substitute for the mother, except by taking her place. By suppressing her to take her place.'[20]

However, if Brontë rejects the notion of the heroine replacing the mother, in the sense of 'taking her place', what she does in the end, I would argue, is replace the mother, providing in the imagination precisely the substitute that is impossible in reality. As I will go on to argue in the next two chapters, in the depiction of Jane's relationship with Rochester at Ferndean, Brontë creates a fantasy of sexual and maternal fusion. In her stress on Jane's kinship and oneness with Rochester, Brontë retreats from the painful implications of the fundamental dilemma of the subject's desire for union and need for separateness into the Imaginary wholeness of the pre-Oedipal state. Indeed, perhaps part of the novel's lasting attraction is that it holds up as possible the kind of fantastic symbiosis which, as Charlotte's sister Emily recognised in *Wuthering Heights*, was tragically impossible in a world of adult sexuality.

2

Sexuality

In a vehement denunciation of the position of middle-class women in 1852, Florence Nightingale protested that the women of England were consistently denied any satisfaction of their 'passion, intellect and moral activity', and that they collaborated with the subversion and denial of their sexuality by going about 'maudling to each other and preaching to their daughters that "women have no passions"'.[1] A sense of this oppression, which Nightingale compared to the practice of binding Chinese women's feet, is deftly created in the opening scenes of *Jane Eyre*. As I have argued elsewhere, the early chapters, while sketching the plight of the orphan Jane, also suggest emblematically an array of constrictions faced by women of the period. The novel opens with Jane's retreat to the 'double retirement' of the breakfast-room window seat in an attempt to render herself invisible in the hostile environment of Gateshead. Her trespass in this case is to be found reading John Reed's books with which, he asserts, she has 'no business'. Thus she is forbidden access to the knowledge of books, which might offer her the liberation of 'draw[ing] parallels' and hence the ability to contextualise and generalise from her experience. Doubly powerless as a girl child and an orphan, Jane is forced to endure the bullying and violence that John Reed, as favoured son, inflicts with impunity. Repeatedly, her lot is to be confined, most dramatically in the terror of the red-room. In that decisive episode the servants threaten to tie her to a chair – using, significantly enough, a pair of female garters for binding. Jane escapes such bondage only by promising that she 'will not stir' (12). In all, then, invisibility, ignorance, passivity, restraint, submission and stillness are the strictures that Jane, like so many of her sisters, faces in the home. Indeed, the conditions that Mrs Reed stipulates for her release from the red-room – 'it is only on condition of perfect submission and stillness that I shall liberate you' (18) – echo the exhortation to all English women to 'suffer and be still'. It is not surprising, therefore, that *Jane Eyre* caused a sensation when it appeared in such a climate in 1847, burning as it was with 'an ungodly discontent', and giving voice to a rhetoric of rebellion and passionate self-affirmation:

> It is vain to say human beings ought to be satisfied with tranquillity: they must have action; and they will make it if they cannot find it. Millions are condemned to a stiller doom than mine, and millions are in silent revolt against their lot. Nobody knows how many rebellions besides political rebellions ferment in the masses of life which people earth. Women are supposed to be very calm generally: but women feel just as men feel; they need exercise for their faculties, and a field for their efforts as much as their brothers do; they suffer from too rigid a restraint, too absolute a stagnation, precisely as men would suffer; and it is narrow-minded in their more privileged fellow-creatures to say that they ought to confine themselves to making puddings and knitting stockings, to playing on the piano and embroidering bags. It is thoughtless to condemn them, or laugh at them, if they seek to do more or learn more than custom has pronounced necessary for their sex. (111)

Jane Eyre has justifiably been hailed by earlier feminist critics, then, as a ground-breaking text which – contrary to the effacement and denial of women's sexual identity prevalent in so much of the life and literature of mid-nineteenth-century England – asserted not only that women experienced sexual passion, but also that they had a right to expect sexual fulfilment. Just as Brontë resisted the double standards of contemporary literary critics who insisted on judging her 'as a woman', not 'as *an* author', so too, in *Jane Eyre*, she challenged the hypocrisy which represented sexual desire as alien to women. Thus, for example, when Rochester torments Jane with the prospect of his marriage to Blanche Ingram, Jane confronts the cruelty of his underestimation of her passion:

> 'Do you think I can stay to become nothing to you? Do you think I am an automaton? – a machine without feelings? . . . I have as much soul as you, – and full as much heart! And if God had gifted me with some beauty, and much wealth, I should have made it as hard for you to leave me, as it is now for me to leave you.' (256)

Similarly, Jane's final resolve to refuse St John's proposal of marriage stems from a frank recognition of sexual repugnance. To 'endure all forms of love' without desire would, she insists, be 'monstrous': 'my sense, such as it was, directed me only to the fact that we did not love each other as man and wife should; and therefore it inferred we ought not to marry' (410).

As well as asserting an equality of masculine and feminine desire in *Jane Eyre*, Charlotte Brontë also sought to envision an equality of power within a heterosexual relationship. Throughout the novel she makes constant play of a shifting dynamic of mastery and submission. So, on the one hand, Jane claims that 'Mr. Rochester had such a direct way of giving orders, it seemed a matter of course to obey him promptly' (131); yet on the other she refers frequently to her 'sense of power over him' (268). Similarly, whereas her sense of him as 'master' pervades the whole novel, he concedes that she has a unique hold over him: 'I never met your likeness, Jane: you please me, and you master me' (263).

Jane's discovery of her inheritance at the end of the novel provides the conventional *volte face* to balance in some degree the economic inequality between the pair, and Rochester's physical supremacy, which is underscored throughout by his repeated threats of violence, both figurative and literal, is effectively – if crudely – nullified by his maiming in the Thornfield fire. The apparent arbitrariness of this equalising impulse in the novel's ending is better understood when it is seen as 'the last of a sequence of similar impulses which have been employed throughout the novel'.[2] In Jane's first meeting with Rochester on the icy road above Thornfield she must lend him support as he is temporarily 'maimed' by his sprained ankle, and she does so free from any awareness of his identity as her employer and master of Thornfield Hall. Rochester's physical vulnerability is repeated in the scene where Jane saves him from immolation in the blaze that Bertha sets around his bed. Further, many of the important interchanges between Jane and Rochester take place out of doors in a natural world divorced from the trappings of Rochester's power, and even at moments when his economic superiority is most clearly evident – as when he launches on a spending spree to provide a lavish trousseau for Jane – Brontë's heroine insists on her financial independence: 'I shall continue to act as Adèle's governess: by that I shall earn my board and lodging, and thirty pounds a year besides. I'll furnish my own wardrobe out of that money, and you shall give me nothing' (272).

Jane Eyre, then, lends itself in many respects to a 'heroic' reading of its treatment of sexuality, given the forceful claims it makes for women's sexual identity, for their 'desire to desire', and for a vision of equality in sexual politics. However, even such heroic readings have acknowledged a sense of ambivalence in Brontë's exploration of female sexuality, though they have tended to regard it as peripheral. In the remainder of this chapter, however, I want to shift that focus and treat Brontë's ambivalence as central, tracing in it the operation of fear, disgust and guilt. I shall argue that the nature of Jane's relationship with Rochester at the end of the novel allows Brontë to transform and evade threatening questions of sexuality, creating instead a mythic fusion between her protagonists which banishes considerations of adult sexuality.

For all Jane's declarations of 'blissful union' (289) with Rochester, the language of their relationship is permeated by a note of struggle and fear. Similarly, the images Jane resorts to are revealingly combative. So, she speaks of Blanche Ingram's efforts at fascinating Rochester as 'arrows that continually glanced off from Mr. Rochester's breast and fell harmless at his feet', and contemplates that if shot by her 'surer hand', they would have 'quivered keen in his proud heart' (189). Again, she describes crushing Rochester's hand, which was 'ever hunting' her own (271). In the contest to 'subdue and rule' (423) Jane recognises that 'submission' in her would only foster 'despotism' in him (276). There is no doubt that the struggle is titillating for Jane: 'I knew the pleasure of vexing and soothing him by turns; it was one I chiefly delighted in, and a sure instinct always prevented me from going too far: beyond the verge of provocation I never ventured; on the extreme brink I liked well to try my skill' (160). However, as she herself concedes, 'though not without its charm', the combat was 'perilous' (306).

This sense of peril is further underscored by the metaphorical violence that characterises so much of the language of their relationship. Rochester's declarations of love – 'When once I have fairly seized you, to have and to hold, I'll just – figuratively speaking – attach you to a chain like this' (273) – are scarcely less aggressive than his expressions of exasperation: 'What good would it do if I bent, if I uptore, if I crushed her? . . . If I tear, if I rend the slight prison, my outrage will only let the captive loose' (322). Similarly, Jane's descriptions of Rochester's 'irate and piercing' (122) eyes, which seem to 'dive into' (134) her own, suggest a kind of assault.[3]

Possession and power are the currency of the relationship between Jane and Rochester. Accordingly, jealousy, which is concerned more with ownership than with love, plays an important role in *Jane Eyre*, and indeed in all of Charlotte Brontë's novels, serving variously as a catalyst and a means of control in the sexual dynamic between them. So, it is Rochester's 'best ally' (265) when he plays upon Jane's fears about Blanche Ingram to elicit a declaration from her, just as it is a welcome tool for Jane when she encourages Rochester to regard St John as a rival in order to 'fret' him out of his melancholy.

In a relationship which is far from 'blissful', then, it is not surprising to find that, contrary to the mutuality claimed for it, the dynamic between Jane and Rochester is remarkably manipulative. Rochester's attempt to deceive Jane into marrying him – 'I wanted to have you safe before hazarding confidences' (319) – provides perhaps the most dramatic example of manipulation, but even in moments of high passion, as in their confrontation after the discovery of Bertha's existence, Jane calculates her responses in an effort to maintain control:

> I had been struggling with tears for some time: I had taken great pains to repress them, because I knew he would not like to see me weep. Now, however, I considered it well to let them flow as freely and as long as they liked. If the flood annoyed him, so much the better. So I gave way, and cried heartily. (307)

Jane's struggle to resist possession and maintain control is indeed 'perilous', and, ironically, what compounds her fear immeasurably is her desire. Dependence is threatening for Jane precisely because, in part, she wants it; she desires 'a master', someone to be her 'whole world', a partner from whom she is indistinguishable, 'bone of his bone and flesh of his flesh'.[4] And behind her preoccupation with asserting her autonomy and identity – 'I will be myself' (262), 'I am Jane Eyre' – lies the spectre of Rochester's metaphorical and literal obliteration of Bertha's subjecthood: 'Let her identity . . . be buried in oblivion' (313), and the nagging fear that sexual relationship threatens the annihilation of the ego.

This threat finds further expression in the novel in a web of connections suggested between sexuality and death. The glimpse of the 'boudoir' at Thornfield, for example, with its crimson couches and ottomans glowing 'in rich contrast' to the white carpet and ceiling, creates an effect of 'the general blending of snow and fire' (105) which recalls the distinctive red and crimson decor of the deathly red-room at Thornfield. Jane's lapse into unconsciousness through a fit of terror in the first red-room is repeated when she is figuratively on the threshold of the second – that is, on the eve of her wedding. Her second collapse is provoked, of course, by the monstrous apparition of Bertha tearing her bridal veil, but perhaps Bertha's action merely embodies, in some ways, Jane's own reluctance in facing her wedding day. The language with which Jane describes the advent of her nuptials is strikingly negative:

'The month of courtship had wasted: its very last hours were being numbered. There was no putting off the day that advanced – the bridal day' (277).[5]

Further, Jane contemplates the macabre thought that her new identity as 'Mrs Rochester' might be 'still-born': 'I would wait to be assured she had come into the world alive, before I assigned to her all that property' (277) – an image which not only indicates her resistance to the threatened loss of identity but also suggests a link between her bridal – or sexual – self and death. Accordingly, Jane's costume is described as 'strange, wraith-like apparel' (278), and she arrives at the church with her face bloodless, her 'cheeks and lips cold' (291). As though her 'usual self' had been extinguished, Jane perceives her reflection in the mirror of her bedroom only as 'the image of a stranger' (289). That sense of self-extinction is further highlighted by the disconcerting passivity with which she proceeds through the day:

> I felt weak and tired. I leaned my arms on a table, and my head dropped on them. And now I thought: till now I had only heard, seen, moved – followed up and down where I was led or dragged – watched event rush on event, disclosure open beyond disclosure. (298)

Jane's fear at the threatening aspect of sexuality is compounded by a certain disgust at its expression. The primary focus for that disgust is the figure of Bertha Mason, who haunts the house, and the novel, as the spectre of appetite run wild. It is clear that it is not her madness *per se* that makes Bertha repulsive, for Rochester repudiates Jane's charge to that effect: 'Your mind is my treasure, and if it were broken, it would be my treasure still: if you raved, my arms should confine you, and not a strait waistcoat – your grasp, even in fury, would have a charm for me. . . . I should not shrink from you with disgust as I did from her' (305). It is, rather, Bertha's licentiousness which is cause for revulsion:

> What a pigmy intellect she had – and what giant propensities! How fearful were the curses those propensities entailed on me! Bertha Mason, – the true daughter of an infamous mother, –

dragged me through all the hideous and degrading agonies which must attend a man bound to a wife at once intemperate and unchaste. (310)

The all-consuming nature of Bertha's appetite is stressed by her connection in the novel with fire and with vampirism, and the horror of her sexuality is emphasised by her repeated association with bestiality. So she is revealed to the appalled members of the wedding party as scarcely distinguishable from a beast: 'it grovelled, seemingly, on all fours; it snatched and growled like some strange wild animal: but it was covered with clothing; and a quantity of dark, grizzled hair, wild as a mane, hid its head and face' (295).

There is some danger, of course, that the hero as suitor, then husband, of this vile monster of lust might be tainted by the association. However, while Rochester relates the tale of Bertha's debasement to Jane, he takes care to distinguish (somewhat sophistically, one might think) his own lusts from the likes of Bertha's:

Disappointment made me reckless. I tried dissipation – never debauchery: that I hated, and hate. That was my Indian Messalina's attribute: rooted disgust at it and her restrained me much, even in pleasure. Any enjoyment that bordered on riot seemed to approach me to her and her vices, and I eschewed it. (315)

Jane, too, is not entirely safe from association with Bertha. Not only is she the only person in the novel who repeatedly hears Bertha's maniacal laugh, as though some special connection or communication exists between them, but her past life suggests a parallel capacity for passionate excess. As a child Jane presents 'such a picture of passion' (11) that she is regarded as a 'mad cat' and Miss Abbot, who seeks to restrain her, is 'incredulous of [her] sanity' (12). Similarly, in her 'repulsive' violence the young Jane appears to Mrs Reed as 'a compound of virulent passions, mean spirit, and dangerous duplicity' (18) – a description which is eerily applicable to Bertha. Nor is the sense of affinity suggested by Jane's 'madness' in giving her 'furious feelings uncontrolled play' (38) able to be safely consigned to her past, since in her desire to be with Rochester after the discovery of Bertha's identity Jane finds herself 'insane – quite insane: with my veins running fire, and my heart beating faster than I can count its throbs' (322).

However, for all that the link between Jane and Bertha exists, and has been taken by earlier feminist critics like Sandra Gilbert and Susan Gubar to suggest a depth of passion and anger in the heroine, there is much in the novel which sets Jane up as Bertha's antithesis in a position so removed from desire and corporeality that it almost represents a repudiation of sexuality itself rather than – more simply – an affirmation of difference.

Even before he meets Jane, Rochester's definition of the desirable partner turns on the essential requirement that she should be Bertha's opposite: 'I longed only for what suited me – for *the antipodes* of the Creole' (315; emphasis added). And in Jane he finds the dichotomy perfectly established:

> That is *my wife*. . . . And *this* is what I wished to have (laying his hand on my shoulder): this young girl, who stands so grave and quiet at the mouth of hell, looking collectedly at the gambols of a demon. I wanted her just as a change after that fierce ragout. Wood and Briggs, look at the difference! Compare these clear eyes with the red balls yonder – this face with that mask – this form with that bulk. (297)

Against Bertha's gross corporeality – 'big', 'corpulent', and 'virile' – or even in contrast to Blanche Ingram's insistent physicality – 'Tall, fine bust, sloping shoulders; long graceful neck; olive complexion, dark and clear; noble features; eyes . . . large and black' (161) – Jane is repeatedly presented as diminutive, 'childish and slender' (317), with 'small, slight fingers' (438), 'a little small thing, they say, almost like a child' (432). While this contrast, along with Rochester's descriptions of her as his 'good little girl' and a 'Neophyte, that have not passed the porch of life' (137), who has 'lived the life of a nun' (124), might indicate that Jane is simply sexually uninitiated, there is a good deal in the novel to suggest that she is not so much on the verge of adult sexuality as *beyond* it. So, when Rochester characterises Jane's beauty as 'just after the desire of my heart, – delicate and aerial' (261), he stresses an ethereal quality that effectively desexualises her. It is as though as 'elf', 'fairy', 'changeling' or 'unearthly thing' Jane has been liberated from the 'corruptible . . . cumbrous frame of flesh' (59) which, Helen Burns laments, is humankind's lot. Jane's identity, then, is stressed in terms of spirit, not body, effectively curbing Rochester's desire: 'If I dared, I'd touch you, to see if you are a substance or a shadow, you elf! – but I'd as soon offer to take hold of a blue *ignis fatuus* light in a marsh' (247).

Beyond the diminutive and ethereal quality of Jane's physical stature, her restrained disposition further wards off the disturbing spectre of unbridled sexual appetite represented by Bertha Mason. She is 'by nature solicitous to be neat' (99), she delights in the smallness of her tiny room at Thornfield, her 'bright little space' and 'safe haven' (99), and she treasures cleanliness and order: 'no speck of the dirt, no trace of the disorder I so hated, and which seemed so to degrade me, [was] left' (345). All seems guaranteed against excess.[6]

In addition, Jane's mode of dress, characteristically a 'Quaker trim . . . all being too close and plain, braided locks included, to admit disarrangement' (130), where 'no article of attire . . . was not made with extreme simplicity' (99), seems to prefigure Lucy Snowe's more self-conscious sexual self-effacement in *Villette*. In both novels the heroines aspire to a shadow-like invisibility, a physical absence, despite the fact that in their intellectual and moral assertiveness they are both spiritually very much present. In this light, it is revealing that one of Jane's most famous declarations of passion and equality culminates in a claim for a distinctively disembodied equity: 'I am not talking to you now through the medium of custom, conventionalities, nor even of mortal flesh: – it is my spirit that addresses your spirit; just as if both had passed through the grave, and we stood at God's feet, equal, – as we are!' (256).

In addition to the qualities in Jane which place her safely outside Bertha's sphere, the polarity between the two women is assured by the fact of Bertha's foreignness. Just as the 'sulphur-steams' of a 'fiery West-Indian night' contrast in Rochester's mind with the wind 'fresh' and 'pure' from Europe (312), so Bertha's madness and licentiousness are inextricably linked to her Creole blood, whereas Jane's sound and chaste nature is the legacy of her English inheritance. Though Bertha is of mixed blood, the daughter of 'Jonas Mason, merchant, and of Antoinetta, his wife, a Creole' (293), her madness is, as we have seen, unequivocally linked to her foreign mother.

Responding to this aspect of the novel, Gayatri Spivak and Penny Boumelha have both offered analyses of its racism, and of the race-blindness of earlier feminist accounts of the book.[7] It is true that Brontë's fiction is on occasion marred by a crude xenophobia, which ascribes inherent superiority to all things British:

> for after all, the British peasantry are the best taught, best mannered, most self-respecting of any in Europe: since those days I have seen paysannes and Bäuerinnen; and the best of them seemed to me ignorant, coarse, and besotted, compared with my Morton girls. (394)

However, there is more at stake in this than simple racism. Bertha's monstrous appetite is not merely the pole against which Jane's restraint is defined and measured, it is symptomatic of a characteristic impulse in Brontë's work to define libidinal drive as Other, or foreign to the self. So in her first novel, *The Professor*, for example, sexual desire is consistently constructed as alien, seen either as the domain of foreigners like Mlle Reuter and M. Pelet or imaged as foreignness when it appears in the protagonist, Crimsworth: 'I felt at once barbarous and sensual as a pasha'.[8] The impulse persists in *Jane Eyre* where, beyond the connection between Jamaica and excess, the Continent is also constructed as the locale of the illicit and the debased. Rochester proposes that Jane live as a kept woman in a 'pleasure-villa' in Marseilles (364); the 'slime and mud of Paris' (146) is contrasted against the 'healthy heart of England' (364); and Rochester's trail of dissipation has not defiled English soil but traversed the capitals of Europe, where his list of mistresses – the French Céline, the Italian Giacinta and the German Clara – reads like a checklist of continental laxity.

Similarly, when Rochester becomes exuberant at the prospect of his imminent possession of Jane as his wife, he is described as a 'sultan' bestowing 'on a slave his gold and gems' (271). Jane, however, repudiates his designs, and she does so – revealingly – by characterising them quite explicitly as alien:

> The eastern allusion bit me again: 'I'll not stand you an inch in the stead of a seraglio,' I said; 'so don't consider me equivalent for one: if you fancy for anything in that line, away with you, sir, to the bazaars of Stamboul without delay; and lay out in extensive slave-purchases some of that spare cash you seem at a loss to spend satisfactorily here.' (272)

Fear, aversion and denial, then, may be the obverse of the more celebrated claims for the heroine's sexual assertiveness in *Jane Eyre*. It is not surprising, in the light of this, to find an impulse in the heroine to maintain control through manipulation – or, likewise, moments in the novel where, rather than affirming her sexual identity, the heroine simply evades passionate exchanges. So, for example, when Jane finds Rochester's face 'all kindled, and his full falcon-eye flashing, and tenderness and passion in every lineament', she quails momentarily: 'then I rallied. Soft scene, daring demonstration, I must not have; and I stood in peril of both: a weapon of defence must be prepared' (275). Or, similarly, in an encounter where Rochester desperately seeks to detain Jane, described in language highly suggestive of sexual arousal – 'Up the blood rushed to his face; forth flashed the fire from his eyes; erect he sprang: he held his arms out' – her response is once again retreat: 'I evaded the embrace, and at once quitted the room' (323).

More significantly, Jane psychologically evades her part in desire by stressing her freedom from responsibility in her declarations of passion and longing. When she declares that she feels she belongs with Rochester, for example, it is ostensibly against her will:

> I got over the stile without a word, and meant to leave him calmly. An impulse held me fast, – a force turned me round: I said – or something in me said for me, and in spite of me: –

64

'Thank you, Mr. Rochester, for your great kindness. I am
strangely glad to get back again to you; and wherever you are is
my home, – my only home.' (248)

And when she confesses that she cannot bear to be separated
from him, she does so 'almost involuntarily; and with as
little sanction of free will, my tears gushed out' (254). This
form of analysis of Jane's actions, taken along with her pro-
fessed disposition to obey and her desire to be 'mastered',
has the effect of obviating the element of agency in her desire
– and hence assuaging potential feelings of guilt for that
desire.

The expression of adult sexuality depends upon separateness; its goal is the achievement of union, not fusion, the
'creative encounter of opposites rather than their annihilation'.[9]
It was this paradox of separation and union that Emily Brontë
understood very well and, as I shall argue, that Charlotte sought
to evade. In *Wuthering Heights* the harmony of Catherine and
Heathcliff's bond exists only outside the parameters of adult
sexuality – in childhood or after death. Their metaphysical
oneness, which Emily Brontë insists upon uncompromisingly
with Catherine's declaration: 'Nelly, I am Heathcliff', renders
the possibility of its expression in conventional sexual terms
both inappropriate and inadequate. Hence the novel demonstrates the disruptive effect of puberty on Catherine and
Heathcliff's relationship, and the peculiarly thwarted and
frustrated nature of their passionate exchanges in maturity.
However, contrary to Adrienne Rich's claim that Charlotte
Brontë wrote 'the life story of a woman who is *incapable* of
saying *I am Heathcliff* . . . because she feels so unalterably
herself',[10] I would argue that Charlotte does posit a similar
oneness between her protagonists, but that she seeks to go even
further and present it in the context of adult sexuality and
conjugal bliss. She can do so only by resorting to fantasy,
concluding her novel with a mythic symbiosis between her
hero and heroine, a retreat to an Imaginary undifferentiated
state where the sexual and maternal are merged. This ending,
as I shall go on to argue, far from constituting an assertion of

mature sexual identity, actually represents a regressive evasion and repudiation of it.

I discussed in Chapter 1 the fundamental dilemma of the subject's desire for union and need for separateness in relation to the mother, and considered the way in which the first state promises security and comfort but threatens immersion and self-erasure, while the second promises separateness and self-identity but threatens the pain of loss and loneliness. That dilemma is played out, and finally evaded, in Brontë's depiction of Jane's relationship with Rochester. In many respects Rochester seems to offer Jane a sufficient degree of difference to ensure the security of separateness in the relationship, and not threaten her identity with 'oblivion'. His maleness provides an animating force to the 'uniform and too still existence' (117) of the female inhabitants of Thornfield. His substantial physical bulk opposes her ethereal, diminutive frame, and his worldly experience is contrasted with her sheltered innocence: 'Strange that I should choose you for the confidant of all this, young lady: passing strange that you should listen to me quietly, as if it were the most usual thing in the world for a man like me to tell stories of his opera-mistresses to a quaint, inexperienced girl like you!' (144).

Against the sense of security in difference, however, there are suggestions that difference is not only undesirable, but dangerous. Jane recognises, for example, that Adèle is disadvantaged by her unlikeness to Rochester: 'I sought in her countenance and features a likeness to Mr. Rochester, but found none. . . . It was a pity: if she could but have been proved to resemble him, he would have thought more of her' (146). More significantly, St John's pronounced difference from Jane – he is 'cold' and 'ice' where she is 'hot' and 'fire' (388) – is the basis for an ominous confrontation that Jane sees as potentially fatal:

> I daily wished more to please him, but to do so, I felt daily more and more that I must disown half my nature, stifle half my faculties, wrest my tastes from their original bent, force myself to the adoption of pursuits for which I had no natural vocation. . . .

> The thing was as impossible as to mould my irregular features to his correct and classic pattern, to give to my changeable green eyes the sea blue tint and solemn lustre of his own. (403)

She recognises that to marry such an opposite would 'soon kill' her (416).

Against this, Rochester explains his intention to marry Jane on the grounds that she is 'my equal . . . and my likeness' (257). This affinity is not, however, simply the happy concurrence of sympathies and tastes of the kind Jane shares with the Rivers sisters – 'I liked to read what they liked to read: what they enjoyed delighted me; what they approved, I reverenced' (354) – for, more than likeness, it is in fact sameness that apparently guarantees the success of Jane's and Rochester's relationship. Accordingly, their relationship is repeatedly imaged in terms of physical oneness or fusion. Rochester's talk of their being attached by 'a string somewhere under my left ribs, rightly and inextricably knotted to a similar string situated in the corresponding quarter of your little frame' (254) is suggestive of an umbilical connection, just as Jane's later claim that no woman was 'ever nearer to her mate than I am: ever more absolutely bone of his bone, and flesh of his flesh' (456) suggests a natal rather than marital bond. Similarly, Rochester speaks of a 'pure, powerful flame' that 'fuses' Jane with himself, while in a parallel image of bodily fusion Jane describes the way in which her heart and eyes 'both seemed migrated in Mr. Rochester's frame' (290), perhaps prefiguring the reunion with Rochester at the end of the novel where her body functions on behalf of his:

> I was then his vision, as I am still his right hand. Literally, I was (what he often called me) the apple of his eye. He saw nature – he saw books through me; and never did I weary of gazing for his behalf. (456)

In all, then, their relationship is perceived as quite literally symbiotic: 'in his presence I thoroughly lived; and he lived in mine' (442).

This insistent sense of physical oneness is complemented by

similar claims for an emotional and psychic fusion. Jane repeatedly characterises Rochester as 'her kind': 'I understand the language of his countenance and movements: though rank and wealth sever us widely, I have something in my brain and heart, in my blood and nerves, that assimilates me mentally to him' (177). Predictably, Rochester is seen as capable of reading Jane's unspoken thoughts 'with an acumen to me incomprehensible' (248), and the distinction between self and other is nullified as she finds Rochester, even in disguise, 'as familiar to me as my own face in the glass – as the speech of my own tongue' (204).

Jane's relationship, then, is not concerned with the harmonious management of difference and union, but is posited on a desire for fusion and non-difference. In this sense it is possible to see Rochester existing not so much as a father figure but in some senses as a mother figure.[11] That is to say, the novel's final relationship is a fantasy of an undifferentiated, dyadic relationship where disturbing divisions of self and other have been obliterated, the complete antithesis of the conception of mature sexuality outlined by Luce Irigaray:

> Love is either the mode of becoming which appropriates the other to itself by consuming it, introjecting it into the self until it the self disappears. Or love is the movement of becoming that allows the one and the other to grow. For such love to exist, each one must keep its body autonomous. One must not be the source of the other, nor the other of the one.[12]

In psychoanalytic terms the novel's final relationship belongs in the realm of the pre-Oedipal Imaginary, the domain of the all-nurturing, all-powerful 'phallic mother'. Such a figure exists in fantasy, according to Irigaray, as 'all protective, the ultimate amorous recourse, the refuge against abandonment'[13] – a description which accurately suggests the role Rochester fulfils for Jane at the end of the novel.

In keeping with a notion of the phallic mother as 'haven, refuge and shelter',[14] Jane sees Rochester's presence as the fundamental factor in her sense of belonging: '. . . wherever you are is my home, – my only home' (248). She longs to continue in the 'shelter of his protection' (249) and, severed from his nurturing presence in her exodus from Thornfield, undergoes a period of literal starvation. For Jane, Rochester is all that her 'bad' mother, Mrs Reed, was not. So, while Mrs Reed regards the infant Jane with unbridled antipathy – 'I hated it the first time I set my eyes on it' (234) – Rochester is 'fond and proud' of her, loving her as 'no one will ever love me . . . again' (364). Whereas Jane has suffered at the hands of Mrs Reed's shamelessly preferential treatment of her children, the position is reversed with Rochester, as she is the beneficiary of his unfair favouritism: 'in my secret soul I knew that his great kindness to me was balanced by unjust severity to many others' (148). During her time at Gateshead Jane can do no right, and her difference provides the occasion of constant offence:

> I was a discord in Gateshead-hall: I was like nobody there: I had nothing in harmony with Mrs. Reed or her children, or her chosen vassalage. If they did not love me, in fact, as little did I love them. They were not bound to regard with affection a thing that could not sympathize with one amongst them; a heterogeneous thing, opposed to them in temperament, in capacity, in propensities; a useless thing, incapable of serving their interest, or adding to their pleasure; a noxious thing, cherishing the germs of indignation at their treatment, of contempt of their judgment. (16)

In marked contrast, Ferndean is a place of complete acceptance and assimilation for her:

> There was no harassing restraint, no repressing of glee and vivacity with him; for with him I was at perfect ease, because I knew I suited him: all I said or did seemed either to console or revive him. Delightful consciousness! It brought to life and light my whole nature. (442)

I referred in Chapter 1 to D. W. Winnicott's contention that the mother's face functions as a mirror which offers the daughter a place to confirm her identity,[15] and I suggested that Jane, in failing to recognise her own image in the red-room mirror, fails to recognise the negative and coercive reflection that Mrs Reed holds up to her as 'repulsive'. Against this, Rochester consistently offers her a different 'reflection', a more positive sense of self:

> believe me, you are not naturally austere, any more than I am naturally vicious. The Lowood constraint still clings to you somewhat; controlling your features, muffling your voice, and restricting your limbs; and you fear in the presence of a man or a brother – or father, or master, or what you will – to smile too gaily, speak too freely, or move too quickly: but in time, I think you will learn to be natural with me. (140)

And in time she comes to accept the image she receives from his face as her true reflection:

> While arranging my hair, I looked at my face in the glass, and felt it was no longer plain: there was hope in its aspect, and life in its colour; and my eyes seemed as if they had beheld the fount of fruition, and borrowed beams from the lustrous ripple. I had often been unwilling to look at my master, because I feared he could not be pleased at my look; but I was sure I might lift my face to his now, and not cool his affection by its expression. (260)

The ending, then, creates the sense of an Imaginary dyad, safe from the threat of otherness that Jane had articulated earlier to St John: 'I know what I feel, and how averse are my inclinations to the bare thought of marriage. . . . And I do not want a stranger – unsympathizing, alien, different from me; I want my kindred: those with whom I have full fellow-feeling' (392). In keeping with this, the house at Ferndean, like the relationship, seems impenetrable to intrusion. With its entrance guarded by iron gates between granite pillars, Jane finds it 'deep buried in a wood', which grew 'so thick and dark . . . about it' that the house is invisible from even a 'very short distance' (435).

In its striking isolation it is reminiscent of Rochester's earlier fantasies not merely of seclusion but of exclusion, when he first expresses to Jane the wish to be 'in a quiet island with only you' (206) and later to 'take mademoiselle to the moon, and there I shall seek a cave in one of the white valleys among the volcano-tops, and mademoiselle shall live with me there, and only me'

(269). This sense of exclusivity is reinforced by the banishment of Adèle in the face of Rochester's all-consuming needs and the effacement of their infant son from the text – both discussed above – and by the virtual disappearance of the Rivers sisters, the 'family' Jane was previously so eager to embrace, who in the end she sees 'alternately, once every year' (457).

The bond between Jane and Rochester can be seen to resemble even further the dyadic union of mother and child in the psychoanalytic Imaginary in the way in which what Jane terms the 'nightmare of parting', opposing it to the 'paradise of union' (258), is imaged graphically in terms of physical rending. So Jane fears being 'sundered' from Rochester, he imagines 'bleeding inwardly' at their separation, and when an internal voice tells Jane she must leave Rochester, it does so in terms of amputation: 'you shall, yourself, pluck out your right eye; yourself cut off your right hand: your heart shall be the victim' (301). In contemplating her departure she reflects that she has 'injured – wounded – left my master' (326). It is not until her return that Rochester becomes 'whole' again, as though reversing his symbolic castration, as Jane becomes for him 'his vision' and 'his right hand' (456).

We have already considered that the figure of the phallic mother can be dangerous – that the power which promises security can also threaten to overwhelm. Brontë avoids this dilemma, however, by presenting Rochester as at once powerful and powerless – or, in symbolic terms, at once phallic and castrated. On the one hand he has the power to satisfy all Jane's needs, he remains her 'master' and he retains the 'same strong and stalwart contour' (436) that associates him with power and potency. On the other, this is tempered by the fact that he is now 'as a child' (452) in his physical dependence, and Jane has the controlling role as mediator between him and the world:

> He saw nature – he saw books through me; and never did I weary of gazing for his behalf, and of putting into words the effect of field, tree, town, river, cloud, sunbeam – of the landscape before us; of the weather round us – and impressing by sound on his ear what light could no longer stamp on his eye. (456)

As this paragraph continues, however, it is clear that Brontë blurs the distinctions between control and service:

> Never did I weary of reading to him; never did I weary of conducting him where he wished to go: of doing for him what he wished to be done. And there was a pleasure in my services, most full, most exquisite, even though sad – because he claimed these services without painful shame or damping humiliation. He loved me so truly, that he knew no reluctance in profiting by my attendance: he felt I loved him so fondly, that to yield that attendance was to indulge my sweetest wishes. (456)

And with a similar merging of the notions of power and power-lessness, Brontë creates an impression of restrained capacity about Rochester. Where earlier images refer to him as 'a fierce falcon' and a 'rough-coated keen-eyed dog' (192), the terminology of the ending remains similar but now incorporates an element of restraint, with Rochester as a 'fettered wild-beast', a 'caged eagle' (436).

Rochester's condition, then, manifests the powerlessness of a strong man, power which is not so much lost as in abeyance – hence the partial recovery of his sight. In this way Brontë not only evades the need to replace the mother in the sense of 'taking her place', by *re*-placing her in the guise of an Imaginary substitute,[16] but she also evades another dilemma – the need to choose between two alternatives, either 'to love a (phallic, masculine) mother or identify with a (castrated, powerless) mother', neither of which is 'an adequate basis for autonomous identity'.[17]

In their earlier banter Rochester speculates upon the preconditions Jane will stipulate before agreeing to marry:

> Why, Jane, what would you have? I fear you will compel me to go through a private marriage ceremony, besides that performed at the altar. You will stipulate, I see, for peculiar terms – what will they be? (272)

In the ending of the novel Brontë does establish peculiar terms indeed – in fact, terms which hold out the promise of 'blissful union' (289), 'permanent conformity' (412), an Imaginary symbiosis which evades the threatening dilemmas of adult sexuality. Never again will Brontë consign her heroine and hero to such an asocial fantasy world – and, revealingly, never again does she so confidently and categorically declare: 'Reader, I married him' (454).

3

Identity

Earlier feminist readings of *Jane Eyre* characteristically saw the novel in terms of a development towards psychic health and wholeness for the heroine. So, for example, Elaine Showalter argues that the division in the heroine is resolved by the end of the novel:

> Brontë gives us not one but three faces of Jane, and she resolves her heroine's psychic dilemma by literally and metaphorically destroying the two polar personalities to make way for the full strength and development of the central consciousness, for the integration of the spirit and body.[1]

Similarly, Gilbert and Gubar see the novel as 'Jane's pilgrim's progress' towards 'maturity' and 'selfhood':

> a story of enclosure and escape, a distinctively female *Bildungsroman* in which the problems encountered by the protagonist as she struggles from the imprisonment of her childhood toward an almost unthinkable goal of mature freedom are symptomatic of difficulties Everywoman in a patriarchal society must meet and overcome: oppression (at Gateshead), starvation (at Lowood), madness (at Thornfield), and coldness (at Marsh End).[2]

I have argued likewise, in an earlier work, that the novel is a triumph of achieved balance for the heroine. Suggesting that she has two crucial lessons of self-control and self-assertion to learn in her growth towards maturity, I have contended that Jane's survival 'depends on her ability to mediate between the potentially destructive extremes of her own character: – between the poles of Reason and Feeling, "absolute submission and determined revolt"'.[3] According to such a reading, Jane must attain a form of self-control which involves not mere repression but 'a complex balance of impulses in a fundamental truth to self'.[4]

Such interpretations construe the character of Jane as a 'fictional ideal' and a feminist 'role model'. Indeed, it is this stress on the genuinely inspirational quality of the work that goes a long way towards explaining the continuing importance of the text for women readers. Brontë's contemporaries were so taken by the 'model' of *Jane Eyre* that it became one of the most imitated works of the period – to the point where the *Westminster Review* called for an end to the reign of 'the daughters direct of Miss Jane Eyre',[5] and George Eliot lamented 'the lavish mutilation of heroes' bodies, which has become the habit of novelists' and felt 'especially sorry that Mrs. Browning has added one more to the imitations of the catastrophe in "Jane Eyre" by smiting her hero with blindness before he is made happy in the love of Aurora'.[6] That emphasis on the heroine as an exemplar has been taken up in recent years by Adrienne Rich, who drew attention to the motivational power of the text in an influential essay in *Ms.* magazine:

> Like Thackeray's daughters, I read *Jane Eyre* in childhood, carried away 'as by a whirlwind'. Returning to Charlotte Brontë's most famous novel, as I did over and over in adolescence, in my twenties, thirties, now in my forties, I have never lost the sense that it contains, through and beyond the force of its creator's imagination, some nourishment I needed then and still need today. . . . *Jane Eyre* has for us now a special force and survival value.[7]

These readings of the novel as *Bildung* depend implicitly on a sense of Jane's linear progression, a progression towards the acquisition of a wholly unified, rational and conscious identity. However, as reading practices informed by post-structuralist and psychoanalytic theory have indicated, there is much in the novel to militate against such a view. Annette Tromly, for example, in her study of Brontë's 'autobiographies', focuses on 'the potential distortions of self-portraiture',[8] and Richard ᴊenevenuto takes issue with accounts of the novel which contend that the work 'is structurally organized to reveal a consistent development – however it be identified – in Jane's progress from orphan to wife'.[9]

The fact of division in the novel is not new, of course, to feminist critics, but early accounts tended to see such division more in terms of tensions that were susceptible to reconciliation, enabling claims for Jane's triumphant acquisition of a mature identity as a 'unified, self-present subject of rationality'.[10] However, it is now possible to see the question of identity – like the issues of motherhood and sexuality – as far more problematic, and to recognise that the novel can be read in such a way as to see Jane not simply as torn, but as radically split. The work, then, can be seen as susceptible to two convincing but opposed readings – the one celebrating reconciliation and wholeness, the other exposing a disharmony and heterogeneity that is finally eliminated only by recourse to fantastical evasion in the novel's ending.

Having offered a heroic reading of the first kind elsewhere,[11] I would like now to focus on the possibilities of examining identity in the novel according to the second kind of reading. To begin with, the very title page heralds a multiplicity of layers of authorship and identity, for behind 'Jane Eyre' the narrator stands 'Currer Bell' the editor, behind whom stands 'Charlotte Brontë' the author. Thus, as Annette Tromly has suggested, the tale is in fact 'thrice-told'.[12] In keeping with this multiple nomenclature, the heroine herself, who on occasions adamantly asserts her single identity, is none the less known in the novel under five separate names – Jane, Joan and Janet Eyre, Jane Elliott and Jane Rochester – indicating that the heroine is indeed a 'heterogeneous thing' (16).

Any confident grasp on a consistent narrative identity is further threatened from the outset by the inconsistency of the Preface. Whereas the narrative voice initially affects a certain humility as an 'obscure aspirant', grateful for the 'indulgent ear' lent to its 'plain tale with few pretensions', it goes on to assume a most authoritative tone in declaiming on ethical standards: 'Conventionality is not morality' (3) and decrying literary tastes: 'I see in him an intellect profounder and more unique than his contemporaries have yet recognized' (4). Such apparent disingenuousness is immediately unsettling, and the effect recurs throughout the novel. So, for example, we might compare Jane's humble declaration: 'though I am a defective being, with many faults and few redeeming points, yet I never tired of Helen Burns' (79) with her truthful but none the less arrogant contention only shortly before that the Reed children 'are not fit to associate with me' (27), and wonder if she is not, chameleon-like, mimicking Helen's mode in her account of their friendship. Similarly, her interjection, 'with deference be it spoken', when describing the difference between Rochester and Richard Mason is entirely rhetorical, for her subsequent characterisations are as confidently assertive as they are categorical: 'the contrast could not be much greater between a sleek gander and a fierce falcon: between a meek sheep and the rough-coated keen-eyed dog, its guardian' (192).

The unsureness created by the multiple identities of the novel's title page and moments of apparent disingenuousness in the narrative voice is further underscored by the repeated stress on duplicity in the opening chapters. Jane is characterised as 'a precocious actress' with 'a tendency to deceit', 'underhand', 'dangerous in her duplicity' and 'a liar' by a succession of accusers. And whereas the emphasis of the narrative is on the injustice of these charges, they none the less find their echo in Rochester's denunciations of Jane's evasiveness (122, 135) and in Jane's own resolutions of concealment. She deceives Rochester – 'I have a veil – it is down: I may make shift yet to behave with decent composure' (247) – just as she assumes a persona to 'avoid discovery' (341) with St John. Jane pampers Rochester 'from motives of expediency' (273), pretends to be pleased in order 'to please him' (288) and makes 'no disclosure' of her experience of telepathic connection with him in order to avoid the potentially 'profound impression on the mind of my hearer' (453). In all, Jane's capacity for manipulation, taken with her tendency towards evasion, must in some respects unsettle any simple identification with the narrator and her tale.

Lucy Snowe, Brontë's final autobiographical narrator, has long been regarded as an 'unreliable' tale-teller – and, not coincidentally, has never been subject to the same kinds of 'heroinisation' as Jane Eyre – but perhaps there is more similarity between the two narrators than is usually recognised. Lucy Snowe seems to taunt the reader with her withholding of information – omitting, for example, to inform us of her recognition of Dr John's true identity and deliberately suppressing the name of the person who gives her the cherished white violets. Jane is similarly guilty of almost gratuitous reticence:

> I desired to be tall, stately, and finely developed in figure; I felt it my misfortune that I was so little, so pale, and had features so irregular and so marked. And why had I these aspirations and these regrets? It would be difficult to say: I could not then distinctly say it to myself; yet I had a reason, and a logical, natural reason too. (99)

Having asserted the existence of such a reason, she simply passes on as though she has created the expectation of an explanation only to deny it.

Jane's 'unreliability' extends, too, to the inconsistency of her judgment. Her claim that on reflection she felt disinclined to blame or judge either Rochester or Blanche Ingram 'for acting in conformity to ideas and principles instilled into them, doubtless, from their childhood' (189) is entirely at odds with her attitude to Brocklehurst, for example, and with her censorious presentation of Blanche Ingram. Similarly, her rhetorical vehemence on the subject of injustice – 'When we are struck at without a reason, we should strike back again very hard; I am sure we should – so hard as to teach the person who struck us never to do it again' (58) – is undercut by the revelation of passive acquiescence that follows almost immediately: 'Many a time I have shared between two claimants the precious morsel of brown bread distributed at tea-time; and after relinquishing to a third, half the contents of my mug of coffee,

I have swallowed the remainder with an accompaniment of secret tears, forced from me by the exigency of hunger' (60).

Jane can be further compared with Lucy Snowe in the way in which elements of her narrative contradict the self-assessment she offers. When Lucy Snowe, for example, contends that she is 'guiltless of that curse, an overheated and discursive imagination', we are left to doubt when she goes on to describe the room where Paulina is seated with her head 'on her pigmy hand' as 'haunted'.[13] Similarly, Jane protests, perhaps too strenuously, that she is 'merely telling the truth' (109), 'the plain truth' (111), yet almost immediately she confesses that her perceptions were coloured: 'all sorts of fancies bright and dark tenanted my mind: the memories of nursery stories were there amongst other rubbish; and when they recurred, maturing youth added to them a vigour and vividness beyond what childhood could give' (113).

Jane, then, is not a 'plain' and unpretentious scribe, offering a documentary account of her life. Rather, she is an accomplished storyteller, weaving a 'spell of fiction' (191) which she knows full well has the power to 'beguile' (191). From her earliest years Jane has demonstrated a passion for storytelling. She remembers with fondness and admiration, for example, that Bessie had a 'remarkable knack of narrative' (39), just as she is later drawn by the 'turn for narrative' of her 'chosen comrade' Mary Ann Wilson (78), and her prejudices are clear in her scandalising preference for 'Revelations and the book of Daniel, and Genesis and Samuel, and a little bit of Exodus, and some parts of Kings and Chronicles, and Job and Jonah' over the Psalms, which she finds 'not interesting' (33).

Jane's narrative repeatedly betrays signs of an inveterate storyteller. She is disposed to exaggerate, claiming implausibly that Brocklehurst pauses for 'ten minutes' (67) mid-homily after declaring that she is a liar, or that Rochester muses for 'ten minutes' (294) in silence at the altar before responding to the revelation of Bertha's existence. Similarly, her description of Brocklehurst is marked by a fairytale-like exaggeration: 'What a face he had, now that it was almost on a level with mine! what a great nose! and what a mouth! and what large prominent teeth!' (32). Her claims that Blanche Ingram forces her to bend 'almost to the breaking of my spine' (191) by crowding her at the window suggests an unlikely gymnastic ability, and her account of the rigours of the Sunday ritual at Lowood is almost comic in its excess:

> A frequent interlude of these performances was the enactment of the part of Eutychus by some half dozen of little girls; who, over-powered with sleep, would fall down, if not out of the third loft, yet off the fourth form, and be taken up half dead. The remedy was to thrust them forward into the centre of the school-room, and oblige them to stand there till the sermon was finished. Sometimes their feet failed them, and they sank together in a heap; they were then propped up with the monitors' high stools. (61)

Jane's overstatement is matched by a tendency to overread. In a single moment, for example, she reads 'Pain, shame, ire – impatience, disgust and detestation' in Rochester's 'large pupil' (143), and she ascribes predictably vicious dialogue – 'What can the creeping creature want now?' (225) – to Blanche Ingram on the strength of her haughty look.

As a child Jane cannot distinguish between fantasy and reality: 'Here I walked about for a long time, feeling very strange, and mortally apprehensive of some one coming in and kidnapping me: for I believed in kidnappers; their exploits having frequently figured in Bessie's fire-side chronicles' (42). Later in her life the same confusion – or fusion – might be said to colour her presentation of Rochester. Jane herself speaks of his existence for her as an 'idea' (299), and that sense of Rochester as her imaginative construction is confirmed by the overwrought or picturesque element that is such a feature of her presentation of him. When Jane first encounters Rochester, she describes the scene 'as in a picture' and concedes that as she watches for his appearance her mind is taken up with 'certain of Bessie's tales wherein figured a North-of-England spirit, called a "Gytrash", which, in the form of horse, mule, or large dog, haunted solitary ways, and sometimes came upon belated travellers, as this horse was now coming upon me' (113). She describes his face as 'like a new picture introduced to the gallery of memory', and 'frames' his departure with lines of poetry. His next appearance to her similarly occurs in the context of a pictorial fantasy she is creating, when she is summoned from the fire in the embers of which 'I was tracing a view, not unlike a picture I remembered to have seen of the castle of Heidelberg, on the Rhine' (120). Jane admits to the partiality of her judgment of Rochester, and her use of the present tense at key moments in their relationship perhaps further suggests a loss of the perspective provided by the past-tense narrative. Rochester contributes in return to the element of fantasy surrounding the relationship by offering a vision of Jane in which he is 'either deluding himself, or trying to delude me' (261).

Jane, as storyteller, is conscious of the need to tailor and shape her tale. In order to make it 'credible' she renders a 'restrained and simplified' account of her life to Miss Temple: 'I infused into the narrative far less of gall and wormwood than ordinary' (71). She knows of the power of fiction to wrap one in 'a kind of dream' (201) and she is impatient with those who do not recognise the skill of narrative: 'There are people who seem to have no notion of sketching a character, or observing and describing salient points, either in persons or things' (106). She is conscious, too, of an interdependence between the teller and the auditor – the 'eagerness of a listener quickens the tongue of a narrator' (201) – and she draws attention to the artifice of narrative with metafictional comment: 'A new chapter in a novel is something like a new scene in a play; and when I draw up the curtain this time, reader, you must fancy you see a room in the George Inn at Millcote, with such large-figured papering on the walls as inn rooms have' (94). In all, then, the novel is not only 'thrice-told' but self-consciously fictive, so that the notion of a fable-like simplicity or 'transparent' narrative – any firm view of the heroine, or of a simple relation between the narrative and experience – becomes much less plausible.

Beyond the unreliability and artifice of Jane's narrative there is, in keeping with the heroine's multiple names, a sense of shifting rather than stable identity in the text. In her repeated address to the reader Jane as narrator not only places a distance between the action of the narrative and its telling, but also adopts a range of different postures or personae. On some occasions the tone is conspiratorial – 'Stay till he comes, reader; and, when I disclose my secret to him, you shall share the confidence' (278) – or solicitous: 'Gentle reader, may you never feel what I then felt' (326). At other moments the narrator becomes defensive – 'Who blames me? Many no doubt; and I shall be called discontented. I could not help it' (110) – even antagonistic: 'It is vain to say human beings ought to be satisfied with tranquillity: they must have action; and they will make it if they cannot find it' (110).

Further, that shifting identity is presented as consistently split in the way in which the autobiographical perspective, continually contrasting past action with present perception, creates what Karen Chase has called 'the doubleness in the narrating "I"'.[14] A sense of divided identity is there, too, in Jane's inclination to represent her thoughts in the form of dialogue. So, for example, when she contemplates leaving Lowood, she asks herself what it is she wants and how she might get it:

> for as I lay down it came quietly and naturally to my mind: –
> 'Those who want situations advertise: you must advertise in the
> —shire Herald.'
>   'How? I know nothing about advertising.' Replies rose smooth
> and prompt now: – (87)

At some moments a strangely disembodied 'voice within me' addresses her in the second person – ' "you shall tear yourself away" ' (301) – while at others the narrator speaks of herself interchangeably in the first and third person: 'I was in my own room as usual – just myself, without obvious change. . . . Jane Eyre, who had been an ardent, expectant woman – almost a bride – was a cold solitary girl again: her life was pale; her prospects were desolate' (298). This sense of a double or multiple self is heightened by Rochester's observation that Jane's features and countenance are 'so much at variance' (125), and by images of an interior and exterior self, such as that provided by his famous lament: 'Whatever I do with its cage, I cannot get at it – the savage, beautiful creature! If I tear, if I rend the slight prison, my outrage will only let the captive loose. Conqueror I might be of the house; but the inmate would escape to heaven before I could call myself possessor of its clay dwelling-place' (322). It is confirmed, too, by Brontë's references to phrenology which, as Karen Chase observes, 'insisted on a radical multiplicity of traits; it was pre-eminently a doctrine of the divided self: it presented character as the complex interaction of competing forces'.[15]

All these features of the narrative, then – its unreliability, its self-conscious fictiveness, its sense of a shifting and split narrative subject – militate against a reading of the novel that simply sees Jane's journey as a triumphant progress towards a self-assured, mature identity. Such a reading depends, in any case, upon a notion of Jane as the mistress of her destiny, and while it is true that she makes decisive and courageous choices in her odyssey, any analysis which constructs Jane as an entirely free and self-determining agent, in keeping with a heroic ideal, does so in the face of her own perception of her actions. Repeatedly, Jane attributes her speech and actions to involuntary and unconscious forces. As with her denial of agency in sexual matters, discussed in Chapter 2, she refers to her speech as 'scarcely voluntary . . . something spoke out of me over which I had no control' (27); her answers 'slipped from my tongue before I was aware' (132), and she finds herself moved to speak by 'something in me . . . and in spite of me' (248). If we challenge the quality of agency or decisiveness in Jane's actions, surely we also challenge in some measure her heroic stature. Further, if we see her as at times a victim of her unconscious, we can begin to understand how she might come to internalise some of the values she ostensibly stands against, so that in an eerie echo of Mrs Reed, for example, she rejoices in Adèle's development into a 'docile, good-tempered and well-principled' companion (456).

Tony Tanner suggests a different kind of emphasis on the heroic qualities of Jane Eyre. He stresses not so much Jane's role as a feminist model as her achievement as the narrator/creator of her own life: 'Jane Eyre has to write her life, literally create herself in writing: the narrative act is an act of self-definition.'[16] Tanner's argument still works within traditional humanist assumptions and, indeed, tends to concur with earlier feminist accounts by arguing that in the end Jane achieves true selfhood, living 'not as some false self or distorted role that other people try to impose on her, but . . . with her own self-created, self-defined identity'.[17] However, Tanner does draw attention to an area of particular interest for feminism – that is, the power assumed in Jane's capacity to tell, and no less to see, her life. In this way the emphasis shifts from Jane Eyre as a recuperable identity, as governess and wife of Rochester, to Jane Eyre as speaking and viewing subject.

Feminist theorists have extensively analysed the way in which speech and vision are crucial to subjecthood, examining the habitual construction of woman as the object or Other of the masculine subject: not speaking but spoken for and about, not seeing but seen. Within literary theory the debate has ranged from the contention at one end of the spectrum that the feminist project is to expose the sex bias of language and to make language adequate to the expression of female experience, to the insistence at the other end that there is no 'feminine' position in language from which to speak. Feminist film theory has examined the ways in which 'in classical Hollywood cinema, the woman is deprived of the gaze, deprived of subjectivity and repeatedly transformed into the object of a masculine scopophiliac desire'.[18] Similarly, as Laura Mulvey has argued in her influential essay 'Visual pleasure and narrative cinema': 'In a world ordered by sexual imbalance, pleasure in looking has been split between active/male and passive/female.'[19]

Film theory's stress on the visual offers particular insights for an examination of *Jane Eyre*, because Brontë's text is so concerned with vision and specularity. Indeed, the novel seems often to privilege sight over speech, setting up a hierarchy of the senses. So it is Mrs Reed's eye, ahead of her voice (36), that stirs Jane's antipathy, and it is the remorse in Rochester's eye that Jane notes before the pity in his voice (302). Jane suggests a preference for communication through vision rather than speech: 'an eager and exacting glance fastened on his face, conveyed the feeling to him as effectually as words could have done, and with less trouble' (358); accordingly, the eye has the power to 'express' (136), the face becomes a 'page' to be 'read' (359), and explanation becomes a matter of 'illustration' (429).[20] So, too, she attempts to resist St John's persuasion not by stopping her ears but by closing her eyes: 'My iron shroud contracted around me: persuasion advanced with slow sure step. Shut my eyes as I would, these last words of his succeeded in making the way, which had seemed blocked up, comparatively clear' (408).

Contrary to the dynamics of representation in film, however, it is possible to argue that *Jane Eyre* reverses in some respects the constrictive model of classic cinema that designates 'a textual model which holds the female voice and body insistently to the interior of the diegesis, while relegating the male subject to a position of *apparent* discursive exteriority by identifying him with mastering speech, vision or hearing'.[21] Jane, in her position as autobiographer, habitually enjoys a perspective on the action by virtue of the past tense and, more particularly, by her repeated association with the position of the viewer rather than the viewed, through which she exists in a position exterior to the action with the power to objectify, at times, even herself.

Jane's connection with the visual takes two principal forms, relating to her role as an artist and her position as a spectator. There is repeated stress on her skill in painting and drawing, with a succession of characters admiring her work. Like her skill in narrative, her artistic skill gives her the power to objectify her reality and the satisfying experience of mastery and control on a number of levels. So, emotionally, she restrains her infatuation for Rochester by painting the two portraits of Blanche Ingram and herself as a form of salutary comparison. Socially, she frequently escapes any feeling of discomfort or inadequacy by turning to her area of expertise. In the hostile environment of Gateshead, for example, on her return to her aunt's deathbed, she 'determined not to seem at a loss for occupation or amusement: I had brought my drawing materials with me, and they served me for both' (235), and after working on a German translation alone in her schoolhouse she takes up her 'palette and pencils, and fell to the more soothing, because easier occupation, of completing Rosamond Oliver's miniature' (375). The role of artist, like that of narrator, gives Jane the power to shape her reality – the power of representation. Indeed, she not only has the capacity to create from nothing, to give reality to something she has not seen in her painting of Latmos (128), but in her painting of Blanche Ingram her imaginative creation *precedes* the reality, which simply conforms to the representation: 'As far as person went, she answered point for point, both to my picture and Mrs. Fairfax's description' (174).

According to Christian Metz, the position of the film spectator affords a sense of unity and mastery: 'Coherence of vision insures a controlling knowledge which, in its turn, is a guarantee of the untroubled centrality and unity of the subject.'[22] Such observation has its relevance for *Jane Eyre*, since the heroine's power comes on many occasions from her command of the gaze. It is, for example, her relentless spectatorship which so unnerves the other inhabitants of Gateshead. The maid, Abbot, describes Jane as a 'tiresome, ill-conditioned child, who always looked as if she were watching everybody' (25), and Mrs Reed remembers with agitation the young Jane's 'continual, unnatural watchings of one's movements!' (234). In fact, there does seem to be a preternatural coolness, particularly in childhood, about Jane's assumption of the spectator's position: 'Sitting on a low stool, a few yards from her arm-chair, I examined her figure; I perused her features'

(36). During the course of the novel she repeatedly takes an onlooker's role, aligning herself with the active pleasure in looking of voyeurism rather than the passive satisfaction in display of exhibitionism:

> No sooner did I see that his attention was riveted on them, and that I might gaze without being observed, than my eyes were drawn involuntarily to his face: I could not keep their lids under control: they would rise, and the irids would fix on him. I looked, and had an acute pleasure in looking. (176)

The scene is typical of Jane's inclination to assume a vantage point and enjoy her advantage as spectator. So, for example, at Thornfield she retires to the window seat, whence she can view the gathering of Rochester's house guests; or, at Moor-House, she takes the opportunity afforded by her position out of focus to scrutinise St John:

> Mr. St. John – sitting as still as one of the dusky pictures on the walls; keeping his eyes fixed on the page he perused, and his lips mutely sealed – was easy enough to examine. Had he been a statue instead of a man, he could not have been easier. He was young – perhaps from twenty-eight to thirty – tall, slender; his face riveted the eye. (349)

The text is highly conscious of the power that lies in scrutiny, tracing the ways in which the heroine finds herself locked in earnest contest with various combatants for the controlling gaze. Between Jane and Mrs Reed there is mutual animosity – Jane's 'look' strikes Mrs Reed 'as offensive' (36), while Mrs Reed's eye stirs 'every antipathy' in Jane (36). In a test of strength, their eyes meet – 'I perused . . . her eye settled on mine' (36) – and each has the power to inflict injury – Jane to 'dart retaliation' (36); Mrs Reed to allow her 'eye of ice' to 'dwell freezingly' on Jane (36). Similarly, Jane describes her ordeal at Lowood when Brocklehurst accuses her of deceit precisely in terms of exposure: 'I, who had said I could not bear the shame of standing on my natural feet in the middle of the room, was now exposed to general view on a pedestal of infamy' (68), and once more the gaze is presented in terms of assault: 'I felt their eyes like burning-glasses against my scorched skin' (66).

With Rochester Jane finds herself once more in visual contest. From the outset she signals her equality with him by meeting his interrogation with 'a keen, a daring, and a glowing eye' (318), and the contest becomes part of the sexual dynamic between them. Rochester's eyes are invasive, 'piercing', 'penetrating', and seeming 'to dive into' Jane's (134), while Jane is equal to the challenge, possessing the power to injure in return: 'With that searching and yet faithful and generous look, you torture!' (258). Finally, of course, Jane's victory over Rochester in this regard is made complete by his blindness at the end of the novel.

Perhaps the most deadly contest that Jane faces for the controlling power of the gaze is with St John. Their encounter is combative from the beginning: 'he took a seat, fixed his blue, pictorial-looking eyes full on me. There was an unceremonious directness, a searching, decided steadfastness in his gaze now, which told that intention, and not diffidence, had hitherto kept it averted from the stranger' (350). While Diana and Mary avert their gaze in deference to Jane's embarrassment, their 'colder and sterner brother continued to gaze, till the trouble he had excited forced out tears as well as colour' (351). After a momentary victory over him – 'I looked up at him: he shunned my eye. I knew his thoughts well, and could read his heart plainly; at the moment I felt calmer and cooler than he: I had then temporarily the advantage of him' (375) – St John acknowledges the worthiness of his opponent: 'There is something brave in your spirit, as well as penetrating in your eye' (379).

Significantly, Jane's power to resist St John's gaze is allied to her power to resist his narrative. She has been in peril of being seduced by his oratory, and the threat is one to her fundamental means of self-definition as teller of her tale, as St John 'assum[es] the narrator's part' (383). At the point where she must escape his thrall, she is weakened by an 'inward dimness of vision' (424). It is an answer to her waiting 'eye and ear', to her entreaty to be 'shew[n]' the path, that prompts Jane to assert her power and silence him: 'I broke from St. John; who had followed, and would have detained me. It was *my* turn to assume ascendancy. *My* powers were in play, and in force. I told him to forbear question or remark; I desired him to leave me: I must, and would be alone. He obeyed at once' (425).

Thus far we have seen on the one hand that Jane Eyre's shifting and split identity militates against a simple heroic reading of the novel, while on the other Jane does establish an authority and presence as speaker/'author' and viewer/artist. That authority rests on her control of both verbal and visual representation, which contrasts markedly with the position of woman diagnosed by film theory, where 'woman's exclusion from symbolic power and privilege . . . is articulated as a passive relation to classic cinema's scopic and auditory regimes – as an incapacity for looking, speaking or listening authoritatively, on the one hand, and with what might be called a "receptivity" to the male gaze and voice, on the other'.[23]

However, I want now to suggest that even this subject position is undermined by the ways in which Jane refuses to speak or to be seen – refusals that parallel the evasions discussed in Chapters 1 and 2. As with the issues of motherhood and sexuality, there are signs of Jane's retreat from identity or subjecthood, and in parallel fashion the question of identity resolves itself in the regressive fantasy of the novel's ending.

If Jane's identity depends on language – as Tony Tanner says, she 'literally create[s] herself in writing'[24] – then the threat of her refusal of language that permeates the text must in some sense be a threat to that identity. What emerges first as an acknowledgment of childish incapacity – 'Children can feel, but they cannot analyze their feelings; and if the analysis is partially effected in thought, they know not how to express the result of the process in words' (24) – becomes more habitual in the adult narrator. Thus, there is a recurring stress on the failure to articulate with expressions like 'no language can describe' (68), 'I cannot precisely define' (99), 'more than words had power to express' (265), and 'I wish I could describe . . . but it is past my power' (356).

This inability to speak is matched at times by an unwillingness to reveal, often for no apparent reason. So, as we have seen, Jane will not offer the 'logical, natural reason' (99) she has for concern about her appearance, nor will she reveal her age after tantalisingly raising the issue – 'now, at a distance of – I will not say how many years' (15) – and she rather arbitrarily decides that her early reflections at Lowood, though at times extraordinarily vivid, are at others 'too undefined and fragmentary to merit record' (49).

In textual terms such reticence constitutes a kind of partial self-effacement. More threatening and conclusive still is Jane's resort to silence. We have already considered the narrative ellipsis that occurs during her eight unrecorded years at Lowood, and it is only one of a number of examples of her strategic silence, which give peculiar resonance to Rochester's fear that Jane is merely 'something that would melt to silence and annihilation' (453).

In psychoanalytic terms, sight and speech are the principal modes of subject differentiation. According to Lacan, for example, the mirror stage heralds the beginning of this differentiation for the infant, who confronts its own reflection in the confirming look of the mother (or Other) as much as in the image of an actual mirror, and perceives itself as a separate, discrete entity and not, as previously, as part of a dyadic continuum. The process of differentiation thus begun is completed through the child's entry into language or the Symbolic order, where the child learns to use the designation 'I', conferring on the self a mythic, unified subjecthood. The consequence of this acquisition of subject identity is the experience of desire, founded on the perception of lack – a lack of that which is not the self but allows the self to be constituted: 'Subjectivity is thus from the very outset dependent upon the recognition of a distance separating self from other – an object whose loss is simultaneous with its apprehension.'[25]

In this scheme of things the child not only sees but, just as importantly, is seen. The look – of the divided self of the mirror's reflection, or of the Mother/Other – confirms the subject identity both in its existence and in its lack. And it is precisely this which Jane Eyre resists. We have already noted her inclination to take up vantage points, but it is worth stressing here that those positions are as important for the opportunity they afford for *not* being seen as for the chance they give for seeing. Jane is, as she herself describes, 'very rarely noticed' (28), and the ethereal language so frequently used to describe her, as well as desexualising her,[26] also suggests her invisibility. So Rochester describes Jane as a 'dream or a shade' (247), and as if this were quite literally true, her 'fascinated glance' at the mirror in the red-room reveals a 'hollow' – 'depth', not surface – in which resides not the confirming look of a reflection of self but an alien image, 'the strange little figure there gazing at me, with a white face and arms specking the gloom, and glittering eyes of fear moving where all else was still' (14). There is a similar repudiation of the self-defining gaze when Jane characterises the reflection in the mirror on her wedding day as 'the image of a stranger' (289).

When Jane describes the idyllic setting of the orchard at Thornfield, the most 'Eden-like' location in the grounds, she does so, significantly, in terms of the shelter it offers from view:

> a very high wall shut it out from the court, on one side; on the other, a beech avenue screened it from the lawn. At the bottom was a sunk fence; its sole separation from lonely fields: a winding walk, bordered with laurels and terminating in a giant horse-chestnut, circled at the base by a seat, led down to the fence. Here one could wander unseen. (250)

Nowhere is Jane's role to see and not be seen more evident than in her reunion with Rochester. Her first glimpse of the blinded Rochester is imaged in explicitly voyeuristic terms: 'I stayed my step, almost my breath, and stood to watch him, myself unseen, and alas! to him invisible' (436), and the effect is continued with her entry for breakfast the following morning: 'Entering the room very softly, I had a view of him before he discovered my presence. It was mournful, indeed, to witness the subjugation of that vigorous spirit to a corporeal infirmity' (444).

While Rochester is a thwarted figure, attempting vainly 'to

see with those sightless eyes' (438), there is, of course, a certain appropriateness in the form of his punishment. Not only is blindness the biblical punishment of the lustful, but in a text which repeatedly privileges the power of sight, it signifies the most telling diminution of power, a connection Rochester makes overtly in his lament: 'My seared vision! My crippled strength!' (449). There is, however, even more at stake in Rochester's blindness. Karen Chase has pointed to the paradox of vision in suggesting that 'what is present (that is, seen) is at the same time absent (that is, distant from the viewer)'.[27] Rochester's sightlessness eradicates this distance between separate entities, and establishes the basis for their continuing relationship: 'Mr. Rochester continued blind the first two years of our union: perhaps it was that circumstance that drew us so very near – that knit us so very close; for I was then his vision, as I am still his right hand' (456). His sight, when it finally returns to one eye, never allows him to see 'very distinctly' (457).

In the end, to see and not to be seen is a fantasy-like usurpation of phallic power. Jane, while not seen, not only sees Rochester but sees *for* him: 'He saw nature – he saw books through me; and never did I weary of gazing for his behalf, and of putting into words the effect . . . of the landscape before us' (456). By allowing Jane this dual vision Brontë creates, then, an effect that is revealingly comparable to the sense of Imaginary wholeness achieved in cinema through the use of a shot/reverse shot technique:

> The shot/reverse shot is generally deemed to be particularly well-suited to this purpose, since the second shot purports to show what was missing from the first shot; together the two shots seem to constitute a perfect whole . . . [and supply] an imaginary version of the absent field.[28]

We have already considered the desire for dissolution, and hence Imaginary wholeness, in Brontë's fantasies of maternal and sexual fusion with Rochester. Once more, in the area of subjecthood or identity, differentiation is evaded in the conclusion with the banishment of the sight that might confer identity.

Conclusion

In conclusion, then, any simple reading of *Jane Eyre* as a feminist *Bildungsroman* tracing Jane's progress from childhood to maturity, from dependence to autonomy or from division to wholeness, is called into question by the 'backward movement of fantasy'[1] which can be traced in the three crucial areas of motherhood, sexuality and identity. Indeed, not only is the sense of linear development illusory, given the regressive and circular movement of Jane's odyssey, but in one sense the beginning of her journey is also an illusion. Jane's 'autobiography' ostensibly offers the reader a tale of origins, but in fact her choice to begin her story in childhood merely highlights a major gap in the text – the silence over her beginnings. We are never offered an account of the formation of Jane's character – in marked contrast, for example, to the presentation of Maggie Tulliver in *The Mill on the Floss*. Instead, we are confronted with a precociously assured ego, an identity that seems substantially at odds with the circumstances that produced it. Brontë's last novel, *Villette*, is similarly vague about Lucy Snowe's early origins, but in that novel there is at least a consistency between the sketchy outline of childhood deprivation and the indelible imprint of repression and deeply internalised scarring that makes Lucy Snowe the difficult character she is. With Jane's mysterious genesis – 'born into [the] world, full grown' (390) – we have, perhaps, no less a sleight of hand in the novel's beginning than in its ending.

Jane's return to Rochester at the end of the novel not only

constitutes a literal turning back but, in terms of the relation-ship envisaged, represents a profound regression. It is a triumph of romance over realism, a choice for a fantasy of completeness and power which involves the forsaking of movement for stasis. Jane has always been a restless, 'roving' character, impatient of 'an uniform and too still existence' (117). It is a quality St John perceives when he notes that her eye 'is not of that description which promises the maintenance of an even tenor in life' (360). Her embrace, then, of a secluded life in a 'desolate spot' (436) 'in the heart of a wood' (304) can be made sense of only in terms of fantasy – the kind of fantasy of contentment that leads Jane to reflect, with the amnesia of nostalgia, 'With little Adèle in my arms, I watched the slumber of childhood – so tranquil, so passionless, so innocent – and waited for the coming day' (289).

The disturbing qualities of Ferndean have frequently been noted. Jane describes it as an 'ineligible and insalubrious sight' (435), while Rochester's conscience recoils from sending Bertha to Ferndean because of 'the unhealthiness of the situation' (304). There is a distinctly death-like air about Jane's ultimate determination – a final resting place in more senses than one. The house, buried in 'the gloomy wood', is barely distinguish-able from the trees, 'so dank and green were its decaying walls' (435). Rochester's presence there makes it for Jane 'my home – my only home' (248), but in the context of Ferndean that designation ironically echoes Helen Burns's description of her impending death as a journey 'to my long home – my last home' (82). Accordingly, the novel closes on Jane's idyll with a funeral benediction from St John. Rather than regard this as a discordant note at the end of a triumphant journey, it is possible to read this preoccupation with death as appropriate to Jane's fantasised retreat into a state of undifferentiated wholeness with Rochester, for that longing to return to a state of Imaginary completeness inevitably involves a longing for the dissolution of the self which is possible only in death.

In the end, then, while earlier feminist claims for Jane Eyre's 'heroic' achievement have some validity, if the contradictions of the text are not to be ignored, they must be juxtaposed against an alternative reading which views Jane's odyssey as a circular movement towards a fantasy of infantile symbiosis and power. Ironically, both readings point to one reason for the novel's enduring fascination for feminists – that is, the enormously seductive power of its fantasies of mature fulfilment in one reading and Imaginary completeness in the other.

Notes

HISTORICAL AND CULTURAL CONTEXT

1. T. J. Wise and J. A. Symington (eds), *The Brontës: Their lives, friendships and correspondence* (Oxford: Shakespeare Head, 1934), I, p. 155. All further references to this work appear in the text abbreviated as *LL*.
2. George Lewes, 'The lady novelists', *Westminister Review*, July 1852, p. 129.
3. Elizabeth Gaskell, *The Life of Charlotte Brontë* (1857; rpt London: Dent, 1971), p. 238.
4. See John Stuart Mill, *The Subjection of Women* (1869; rpt London: Dent, 1982).
5. Quoted in Tillie Olsen, *Silences* (New York: Delta, 1973), p. 233.
6. Barbara Leigh Smith, *A Brief Statement in Plain Language of the Most Important Laws Concerning Women* (London: Chapman, 1854), p. 6.
7. Geoffrey Tillotson, *A View of Victorian Literature* (Oxford: Clarendon Press, 1978), p. 199.
8. *English Woman's Journal*, September 1859, p. 60.
9. Quoted in Elizabeth Gaskell, *Life*, p. 53.
10. Lawrence Dessner suggests that although Brontë's reading was extensive, she had little access to fiction texts; thus her dismissal of all novelists except Scott may have been partly defensive (*The Homely Web of Truth: A study of Charlotte Brontë's novels* [The Hague: Mouton; 1975], p. 14).
11. There is a curious parallel here between Brontë's repudiation of literary paternity/maternity and the creation of her heroine Jane Eyre as precociously and mysteriously full-formed. See discussion, p. 93 below.
12. See Robert Heilman, 'Charlotte Brontë's "New" Gothic', in

96

R. C. Rathburn and M. Steinmann, Jr (eds), *From Jane Austen to Joseph Conrad* (Minneapolis: University of Minnesota Press, 1958), pp. 71–85.

13. Kathleen Tillotson, *Novels of the Eighteen-Forties* (Oxford: Oxford University Press, 1956), p. 149.

14. See Jerome Beaty, 'Jane Eyre at Gateshead: Mixed signals in the text and context', in J. R. Kincaid and A. J. Kuhn (eds), *Victorian Literature and Society* (Athens, OH: Ohio State University Press, 1983), pp. 168–96.

15. Quoted in Elaine Showalter, *A Literature of Their Own: British women novelists from Brontë to Lessing* (1977; rpt London: Virago, 1982), p. 106.

CRITICAL RECEPTION

16. Miriam Allott (ed.), *The Brontës: The critical heritage* (London: Routledge & Kegan Paul, 1974), p. 87. All further references to this work appear in the text abbreviated as *CH*.

17. David Cecil, *Early Victorian Novelists: Essays in revaluation* (London: Constable, 1960), p. 116.

18. Virginia Woolf, *A Room of One's Own* (1928; rpt Harmondsworth: Penguin, 1974), p. 102.

19. F. R. Leavis, *The Great Tradition* (1948; rpt Harmondsworth: Penguin, 1967), p. 37.

20. D. W. Crompton, 'The New Criticism: A caveat', *Essays in Criticism* 10 (1960), p. 362.

THEORETICAL PERSPECTIVES

21. Earl A. Knies, *The Art of Charlotte Brontë* (Athens, OH: Ohio State University Press, 1969), p. ix.

22. Annette Tromly, *The Cover of the Mask: The autobiographers in Charlotte Brontë's fiction* (Victoria, BC: English Literary Studies, University of Victoria, 1982), p. 11.

23. Robert Martin, *The Accents of Persuasion: Charlotte Brontë's novels* (London: Macmillan, 1966), p. 58.

24. Richard Benevenuto, 'The child of nature, the child of grace, and the unresolved conflict of *Jane Eyre*', *English Literary History* 39 (1972), p. 631.

25. Peter Allan Dale, 'Charlotte Brontë's "tale half-told": The

disruption of narrative structure in *Jane Eyre*', *Modern Language Quarterly* **47** (1986), pp. 108–29.

26. Annette Tromly, *The Cover of the Mask*, pp. 14–15.
27. Raman Selden, *A Reader's Guide to Contemporary Literary Theory* (Sussex: Harvester Press, 1985), p. 7.
28. Tony Tanner, 'Passion, narrative and identity in *Wuthering Heights* and *Jane Eyre*', in Susanne Kappeler and Norman Bryson (eds), *Teaching the Text* (London: Routledge & Kegan Paul, 1983), p. 117.
29. Margot Peters, *Charlotte Brontë: Style in the novel* (Madison, WI: University of Wisconsin Press, 1973), p. 4.
30. Karl Kroeber, *Styles in Fictional Structure: The art of Jane Austen, Charlotte Brontë, George Eliot* (Princeton, NJ: Princeton University Press, 1971), p. 4.
31. Robert Heilman, 'Charlotte Brontë's "New" Gothic'.
32. Frederick Ashe, '*Jane Eyre*: The quest for optimism', *Studies in the Novel* **20** (1988), p. 122.
33. Helene Moglen, *Charlotte Brontë: The self conceived* (New York: Norton, 1976), p. 14.
34. Irene Tayler, *Holy Ghosts: The male muses of Emily and Charlotte Brontë* (New York: Columbia University Press, 1990), p. 7.
35. *Ibid.*, p. 10.
36. Annette Tromly, *The Cover of the Mask*, p. 10.
37. Karen Chase, *Eros and Psyche: The representation of personality in Charlotte Brontë, Charles Dickens and George Eliot* (London: Methuen, 1984), p. 3.
38. Mary Poovey, *Uneven Developments: The ideological work of gender in mid-Victorian England* (Chicago: University of Chicago Press, 1988), p. 141.
39. Terry Eagleton, *Myths of Power* (London: Macmillan, 1975), p. 4.
40. Jina Politi, '*Jane Eyre* class-ified', *Literature and History* **8** (1) (1982), pp. 56–66.
41. Marxist–Feminist Literature Collective, 'Women's writing: "Jane Eyre", "Shirley", "Villette", "Aurora Leigh"', in Francis Barker *et al.* (eds), *1848: The Sociology of Literature*, (Colchester: University of Essex, 1978), pp. 185–206.
42. *Ibid.*, p. 186.
43. Adrienne Rich, 'When we dead awaken: Writing as re-vision', in *On Lies, Secrets and Silences: Selected prose 1966–1978* (New York: Norton, 1979), p. 35.
44. Ruth Gounelas, 'Charlotte Brontë and the critics: Attitudes to the female qualities in her writing', *Journal of the Australasian*

Universities Language and Literature Association **62** (November 1984), p. 165.

45. Sandra Gilbert and Susan Gubar, *The Madwoman in the Attic: The woman writer and the nineteenth-century literary imagination* (New Haven, CT: Yale University Press, 1979), p. 73.

46. Adrienne Rich, in *On Lies, Secrets and Silences*, p. 17.

47. Maurianne Adams, '*Jane Eyre*: Woman's estate', in A. Diamond and Lee R. Edwards (eds), *The Authority of Experience: Essays in feminist criticism* (Amherst, MA: University of Massachusetts Press, 1977), p. 140.

48. Adrienne Rich, in *On Lies, Secrets and Silences*, p. 90.

49. Toril Moi, *Sexual/Textual Politics* (London: Methuen, 1985), p. 69.

50. Gayatri Chakravorty Spivak, 'Three women's texts and a critique of imperialism', *Critical Inquiry* **12** (1985), pp. 243–61.

51. *Ibid.*, p. 249.

52. Penny Boumelha, 'And what do the women do? Jane Eyre, Jamaica and the gentleman's house', *Southern Review* **21** (1988), pp. 111–22.

53. Patricia Yaeger, 'Honey-mad women: Charlotte Brontë's bilingual heroines', *Browning Institute Studies* **14** (1986), pp. 11–35.

54. *Ibid.*, p. 15.

55. *Ibid.*, p. 13,

56. Margaret Homans, *Bearing the Word: Language and female experience in nineteenth-century women's writing* (Chicago: University of Chicago Press, 1986), p. 16.

1. MOTHERHOOD

1. Adrienne Rich, *On Lies, Secrets and Silences: Selected prose 1966–1978* (New York: Norton, 1979), p. 91.

2. *Ibid.*, p. 102.

3. Charlotte Brontë, *Jane Eyre*, World's Classics edn (1847; rpt Oxford: Oxford University Press, 1980), p. 29. All further references to this work will appear in brackets in the text.

4. Pauline Nestor, *Female Friendships and Communities: Charlotte Brontë, George Eliot and Elizabeth Gaskell* (Oxford: Clarendon Press, 1985), p. 108.

5. Nancy Chodorow and Susan Contratto, 'The fantasy of the perfect mother', in Barrie Thorne and Marilyn Yalom (eds), *Rethinking the Family: Some feminist questions* (New York: Longman, 1982), p. 65.

6. Elizabeth Grosz, *Sexual Subversions: Three French feminists* (Sydney: Allen & Unwin, 1989), p. 121.
7. Nancy Chodorow, 'Mothering, object-relations, and the female Oedipal configuration', *Feminist Studies* **4** (1978), p. 147.
8. Arguably, this prohibition on feminine hostility to the natural mother is changing. Contemporary women writers are much more likely to accept, even embrace, the anger that was once outlawed:

    > No woman born in this world is immune to the pleasure of being good. We are born to goodness; it is our birthright. Only sheer grit and pigheaded obstinacy make us demand the right to be bad – for we know that only by being bad can we become ourselves – not daughters and granddaughters, but individuals and possibly artists. Being an artist demands a cut umbilicus (which often bleeds); being a daughter demands the cord intact (a bloodless but confining fate). (Erica Jong, *Parachutes and Kisses* [London: Granada, 1984], p. 42)

    Similarly, Karen Elias-Button has argued, in 'The muse as Medusa', that the daughter 'who would mature must defeat her mother. Consequently, many mothers and daughters portrayed in contemporary literature are more embattled than loved' (in C. N. Davidson and E. M. Broner [eds], *The Lost Tradition: Mothers and daughters in literature* [New York: Ungar, 1980], p. 190).
    Contemporary writers, then, have begun to integrate good and bad qualities in their maternal figures, and the ambivalence of their response has become an area of considerable investigation. Freed to a certain extent from the taboo on anger and intent on daughterly self-identification, many contemporary women writers have demonstrated an over-compensatory stress on the oppressive wickedness of the mother. In 'The fantasy of the perfect mother', for example, Nancy Chodorow and Susan Contratto examine three influential texts – Nancy Friday's *My Mother/My Self*, Judith Arcana's *Our Mothers' Daughters* and Dorothy Dinnerstein's *The Mermaid and the Minotaur* – to consider the ways in which an identification with the angry child, together with a belief in total infantile need and maternal responsibility, has 'led to a maternal identification that is in its turn full of rage and fear' (p. 67).
9. Penny Boumelha, 'And what do the women do? Jane Eyre, Jamaica and the gentleman's house', *Southern Review* **21** (1988), p. 114.
10. Nathalie Sarraute, *Childhood* (London: John Calder, 1984), p. 148.

11. See Pauline Nestor, *Charlotte Brontë* (London: Macmillan, 1987), p. 54.
12. Caroline Helstone is the exception in the list of Brontë's motherless heroines, but even here, although her mother makes a miraculous appearance in the heroine's adult life, Caroline Helstone has, to all intents and purposes, grown up motherless.
13. Pauline Nestor, *Charlotte Brontë*, p. 4.
14. Florence Nightingale, 'Cassandra', in Ray Strachey, *The Cause: A short history of the women's movement in Great Britain* (London: Bell & Son, 1928), p. 397.
15. Nancy Chodorow, 'Mothering, object-relations and the female Oedipal configuration', p. 147.
16. Elizabeth Grosz, *Sexual Subversions*, p. 121.
17. Karen Elias-Button, 'The muse as Medusa', p. 200.
18. Ellen B. Rosenman, *The Invisible Presence* (Baton Rouge, LA: Louisiana University Press, 1986), p. 49.
19. For an interesting discussion of the attraction of motherlessness evident in Emily Dickinson's 'murder' of her mother in her poetry, see Barbara Ann Clarke Mossberg, 'Reconstruction in the house of art: Emily Dickinson's "I Never Had a Mother"', in *The Lost Tradition*, pp. 128–38.
20. Elizabeth Grosz, *Sexual Subversions*, p. 123.

2. SEXUALITY

1. Florence Nightingale, 'Cassandra', in Ray Strachey, *The Cause: A short history of the women's movement in Great Britain* (London: Bell & Son, 1928), p. 396.
2. Pauline Nestor, *Charlotte Brontë* (London: Macmillan, 1987), p. 66.
3. In Brontë's last novel, *Villette*, the threatening aspect of masculine sexuality is much more comprehensively depicted; a whole 'language of violation' is built up around the central image of the internal garden of the girls' school, a distinctively feminine inner space that is repeatedly vulnerable, despite taboos, to masculine invasion. For a further discussion of this aspect of *Villette*, see Pauline Nestor, *Female Friendships and Communities: Charlotte Brontë, George Eliot and Elizabeth Gaskell* (Oxford: Clarendon Press, 1985), pp. 132–4.
4. See further discussion, pp. 67–8 below.
5. Brontë's next novel, *Shirley*, is marked by an even more profound

sense of reluctance and gloom surrounding the heroine's impending marriage:

> It had needed a sort of tempest-shock to bring her to the point; but there she was at last, fettered to a fixed day: there she lay, conquered by love, and bound with a vow. . . . Thus vanquished and restricted, she pined, like any other chained denizen of deserts. Her captor alone could cheer her; his society only could make amends for the lost privilege of liberty: in his absence, she sat or wandered alone; spoke little, and ate less. (World Classics edn [1849; rpt Oxford: Oxford University Press, 1981], p. 638)

For a fuller discussion, see Pauline Nestor, *Charlotte Brontë*, pp. 79–80.

6. In this Jane is reminiscent of Brontë's earlier heroine, Frances Henri, in *The Professor*. In that novel the extreme neatness and smallness of Frances's person and environment are stressed as tacit proof of her pleasing restraint, in marked contrast to the excess which characterises the ornate abundance that surrounds the decadent Zoraide Reuter.

7. See Gayatri Chakravorty Spivak, 'Three women's texts and a critique of imperialism', *Critical Inquiry* 12 (1985), pp. 243–61, and Penny Boumelha, 'And what do the women do? Jane Eyre, Jamaica and the gentleman's house', *Southern Review* 21 (1988), pp. 111–22.

8. Charlotte Brontë, *The Professor* (1857; rpt London: Dent, 1980), p. 162.

9. Elizabeth Grosz, *Sexual Subversions: Three French feminists* (Sydney: Allen & Unwin, 1989), p. 170.

10. Adrienne Rich, *On Lies, Secrets and Silences: Selected prose 1966–1978* (New York: Norton, 1979), p. 91.

11. For a contrary view, see Irene Tayler, *Holy Ghosts: The male muses of Emily and Charlotte Brontë* (New York: Columbia University Press, 1990).

12. Quoted in Elizabeth Grosz, *Sexual Subversions*, p. 170.

13. Quoted in *ibid.*, p. 125.

14. *Ibid.*, p. 124.

15. See p. 49 above.

16. See pp. 51–2 above.

17. Elizabeth Grosz, *Sexual Subversions*, p. 119.

3. IDENTITY

1. Elaine Showalter, *A Literature of Their Own: British women*

novelists from Brontë to Lessing (1977; rpt London: Virago, 1982), p. 113.

2. Sandra Gilbert and Susan Gubar, *The Madwoman in the Attic: The woman writer and the nineteenth-century literary imagination* (New Haven, CT: Yale University Press, 1979), p. 339.
3. Pauline Nestor, *Charlotte Brontë* (London: Macmillan, 1987), p. 50.
4. *Ibid.*, p. 50.
5. Quoted in Elaine Showalter, *A Literature of Their Own*, p. 100.
6. George Eliot, 'Belles Lettres', *Westminster Review*, January 1857, p. 306.
7. Reprinted in Adrienne Rich, '*Jane Eyre*: The temptations of a motherless woman', in *On Lies, Secrets and Silences: Selected prose 1966–1978* (New York: Norton, 1979), p. 89.
8. Annette Tromly, *The Cover of the Mask: The autobiographers in Charlotte Brontë's fiction* (Victoria, BC: English Literary Studies, University of Victoria, 1982), p. 15.
9. Richard Benevenuto, 'The child of nature, the child of grace, and the unresolved conflict of *Jane Eyre*', *English Literary History* 39 (1972), p. 622.
10. Chris Weedon, *Feminism and Post-Structuralist Theory* (Oxford: Blackwell, 1987), p. 71.
11. Pauline Nestor, *Charlotte Brontë*.
12. Annette Tromly, *The Cover of the Mask*, p. 14.
13. Charlotte Brontë, *Villette* (1853; rpt Harmondsworth: Penguin, 1981), p. 69.
14. Karen Chase, *Eros and Psyche: The representation of personality in Charlotte Brontë, Charles Dickens and George Eliot* (London: Methuen, 1984), p. 51.
15. *Ibid.*, p. 56.
16. Tony Tanner, 'Passion, narrative and identity in *Wuthering Heights* and *Jane Eyre*', in Susanne Kappeler and Norman Bryson (eds), *Teaching the Text* (London: Routledge & Kegan Paul, 1983), p. 116.
17. *Ibid.*, p. 117.
18. Mary Anne Doane, *The Desire to Desire: The woman's film in the 1940's* (London: Macmillan, 1988), p. 2.
19. Laura Mulvey, 'Visual pleasure and narrative cinema' in G. Mast and C. Cohen (eds), *Film Theory and Criticism* (New York: Oxford University Press, 1985), p. 808.
20. What we might take to be a simple mistake – the claim by the innkeeper that he 'saw |Bertha| and heard her with my own eyes' (433) – perhaps testifies to the unconscious primacy Brontë afforded sight in the novel.

21. Kaja Silverman, *The Acoustic Mother: The female voice in psychoanalysis and cinema* (Bloomington, IN: Indiana University Press, 1988), p. ix. Mary Anne Doane suggests, more generally, that a difference in representation between the forms may be connected to a difference in audience: 'the rise of the novel as the most popular vehicle for the formulation of narrative is usually linked explicitly with a female reading public. . . . Yet, although the cinema is often theorized as the extension and elaboration of the narrative mechanisms of the nineteenth-century novel, its spectator is almost always conceptualized in the masculine mode. It is as though the historical threat of a potential feminization of the spectatorial position required an elaborate work of generic containment' (Mary Anne Doane, *The Desire to Desire*, p. 2).
22. Quoted in Mary Anne Doane, *The Desire to Desire*, p. 15.
23. Kaja Silverman, *The Acoustic Mother*, p. 31.
24. Tony Tanner, 'Passion, narrative and identity', p. 116.
25. Kaja Silverman, *The Acoustic Mother*, p. 7.
26. See p. 62 above.
27. Karen Chase, *Eros and Psyche*, p. 91.
28. Kaja Silverman, *The Acoustic Mother*, p. 12.

CONCLUSION

1. Kaja Silverman, *The Acoustic Mother: The female voice in psychoanalysis and cinema* (Bloomington, IN: Indiana University Press, 1988), p. 85.

Select Bibliography

WORKS BY CHARLOTTE BRONTË

The Brontës: Their lives, friendships and correspondence, ed. T. J. Wise and J. A. Symington, 4 vols (Oxford: Shakespeare Head, 1932).
Emma a Fragment (1860), in *The Professor and Emma a Fragment* (London: Dent, 1980).
Five Novelettes, ed. Winifred Gérin (London: Folio Press, 1971).
Jane Eyre, World's Classics edn (1847; rpt Oxford: Oxford University Press, 1980).
The Miscellanies and Unpublished Writings of Charlotte and Patrick Brontë, ed. T. J. Wise and J. A. Symington, 2 vols (Oxford: Shakespeare Head, 1934).
Poems, by Acton, Ellis and Currer Bell (London: Aylott & Jones, 1846).
The Professor (1857; rpt London: Dent, 1980).
Shirley, World's Classics edn (1849; rpt Oxford: Oxford University Press, 1981).
Tales from Angria, ed. Phyllis Bentley (London: Collins, 1954).
Villette (1853; rpt Harmondsworth: Penguin, 1981).

CRITICAL WORKS

Maurianne Adams, '*Jane Eyre*: Woman's estate', in A. Diamond and Lee R. Edwards (eds), *The Authority of Experience: Essays in feminist criticism* (Amherst, MA: University of Massachusetts Press, 1977). Adams reads the text for its thematic relevance to feminist issues, especially those of emotional and financial dependence.

Miriam Allott (ed.), *The Brontës: The critical heritage* (London: Routledge & Kegan Paul, 1974) and *Charlotte Bronte: 'Jane Eyre' and 'Villette'*, The Casebook Series (London: Macmillan, 1973). Two collections of critical responses to Brontë's work, providing a useful historical overview of fashions and prejudices in criticism.

Peter Bellis, 'In the window-seat: Vision and power in *Jane Eyre*', *English Literary History* 54 (1987), pp. 639–52. Bellis examines the importance of spectatorship in the novel, and argues that the conflict between Jane and Rochester is embodied in a conflict between masculine and feminine modes of vision.

Richard Benevenuto, 'The child of nature, the child of grace and the unresolved conflict of *Jane Eyre*', *English Literary History* 39 (1972), pp. 620–38. A post-structuralist reading which points to the impossibility of reconciling the claims of nature and of grace on Jane's personality.

Penny Boumelha, *Charlotte Brontë* (Hemel Hempstead: Harvester Wheatsheaf, 1990). A Marxist–feminist analysis which examines Jane's co-option into patriarchal capitalist values and challenges the racist and classist assumptions of many feminist readings of the novel.

Karen Chase, *Eros and Psyche: The representation of personality in Charlotte Brontë, Charles Dickens and George Eliot* (London: Methuen, 1984). Chase combines aesthetic and psychological consideration to examine the way in which Brontë's novels give structure to emotion, and how they represent the mind.

Peter Allan Dale, 'Charlotte Brontë's "tale half-told": The disruption of narrative structure in *Jane Eyre*', *Modern Language Quarterly* 47 (1986), pp. 108–29. Dale considers the story in terms of a grammar of narratology and its challenge to the expectations of the competent reader.

Terry Eagleton, *Myths of Power: A Marxist study of the Brontës* (London: Macmillan, 1975). One of the earliest Marxist readings, which argues that Brontë's work is marked by a constant struggle between an individualistic, radical impulse towards protest and rebellion and an affirmation of habits of piety, submission and conservatism.

Elizabeth Gaskell, *The Life of Charlotte Brontë* (1857; rpt London: Dent, 1971). Brontë's friend and fellow novelist Elizabeth Gaskell provides an insightful and compassionate account of Brontë's life.

Winifred Gérin, *Charlotte Brontë: The evolution of genius* (Oxford: Clarendon Press, 1967). Conventional in its approach, but recognised as the authoritative modern biography of Brontë.

S. Gilbert and S. Gubar, *The Madwoman in the Attic: The woman writer and the nineteenth-century literary imagination* (New

Haven, CT: Yale University Press, 1979). An early feminist analysis which reads the text as Jane's pilgrim's progress towards maturity and draws attention to the subversive subtext provided by the story of Bertha Mason.

Robert Heilman, 'Charlotte Brontë's "New" Gothic', in R. C. Rathburn and M. Steinmann, Jr (eds), *From Jane Austen to Joseph Conrad* (Minneapolis: University of Minnesota Press, 1958). An influential essay which examines the way in which Brontë imbues Gothic devices with a new psychological and social force.

Margaret Homans, *Bearing the Word: Language and female experience in nineteenth-century women's writing* (Chicago: University of Chicago Press, 1986). Homans examines women's revisions of the female cultural myth of women's place in language, and considers the way in which Brontë investigates, through her writing, the conflicts between being a daughter and being a writer.

Earl A. Knies, *The Art of Charlotte Brontë* (Athens, OH: Ohio State University Press, 1969). One of the earliest studies to focus on Brontë's prose and the development of her artistry rather than on her capacity as a fictionalised autobiographer.

Robert Martin, *The Accents of Persuasion: Charlotte Brontë's novels* (London: Macmillan, 1966). Martin eschews biography and makes claims for Brontë's comprehensive grasp of her material, which allows for the fusion of disparate parts into a real unity.

Marxist–Feminist Literature Collective, 'Women's writing: "Jane Eyre", "Shirley", "Villette", "Aurora Leigh"', in Francis Barker *et al.* (eds), *1848: The Sociology of Literature* (Colchester: University of Essex, 1978). The writers call for a synthesis of Marxist and feminist thought in order to expose the interdependence between class structure and patriarchy.

John Maynard, *Charlotte Brontë and Sexuality* (Cambridge: Cambridge University Press, 1984). Maynard examines Brontë's presentation of sexuality, and claims that her vision anticipated most of the major assumptions of Havelock Ellis, Freud, and their successors.

Helene Moglen, *Charlotte Brontë: The self conceived* (New York: Norton, 1976). A critical biography which contends that Brontë's novels illuminate her life, and that both offer the reader insights into the modern female psyche and the feminist struggle.

Pauline Nestor, *Charlotte Brontë* (London: Macmillan, 1987). Nestor argues that Jane learns two crucial lessons of self-control and self-assertion in her progress to maturity, and that throughout the novel Brontë endeavours to imagine a heterosexual relationship developing in a context of equal power between men and women.

Nancy Pell, 'Resistance, rebellion and marriage: The economics of *Jane Eyre*', *Nineteenth Century Fiction* **31** (1977), pp. 397–420. Pell examines the way in which the novel offers a social and economic critique of bourgeois patriarchal authority.

Margot Peters, *Charlotte Brontë: Style in the novel* (Madison, WI: University of Wisconsin Press, 1973). Peters combines linguistic analysis and literary criticism in an effort to provide a scientific study of style.

Margot Peters, *Unquiet Soul: A biography of Charlotte Brontë* (London: Hodder & Stoughton, 1975). A psychological study which reads Brontë's life in conjunction with her art as an eloquent protest against the cruel constraints of patriarchy.

Jina Politi, '*Jane Eyre* class-ified', *Literature and History* 8 (1) (1982), pp. 56–66. A Marxist–feminist analysis which argues that Jane's progress is one from rebellious marginality to quiescent conformity.

Mary Poovey, *Uneven Developments: The ideological work of gender in mid-Victorian England* (Chicago: University of Chicago Press, 1988). Poovey reads *Jane Eyre* as a 'hysterical text' which acts out symptomatically what cannot make its way into the psychologically realistic narrative.

Adrienne Rich, '*Jane Eyre*: The temptations of a motherless woman', in *On Lies, Secrets and Silences: Selected prose 1966–1978* (New York: Norton, 1979). An influential early feminist essay which sees Jane's trials as archetypally feminine and points to the sequence of mother figures who populate her pilgrimage and help her on her way.

Elaine Showalter, *A Literature of Their Own: British women novelists from Brontë to Lessing* (1977; rpt London: Virago, 1982). An early feminist reading which sees Jane's journey as a progressive movement towards the resolution of psychic division in the eventual achievement of integration of spirit and body.

Gayatri Chakravorty Spivak, 'Three women's texts and a critique of imperialism', *Critical Inquiry* **12** (1985), pp. 243–61. Spivak exposes the imperialism of Brontë's text and examines the political implications of an unquestioning celebration of Jane's feminist individualism.

Tony Tanner, 'Passion, narrative and identity in *Wuthering Heights* and *Jane Eyre*', in Susanne Kappeler and Norman Bryson (eds), *Teaching the Text* (London: Routledge & Kegan Paul, 1983). Tanner examines the narrative act as an act of self-definition.

Irene Tayler, *Holy Ghosts: The male muses of Emily and Charlotte Brontë* (New York: Columbia University Press, 1990). Tayler examines the creative development of the two sisters in relation to their creation of a male muse.

Select Bibliography

Annette Tromly, *The Cover of the Mask: The autobiographers in Charlotte Brontë's fiction* (Victoria, BC: English Literary Studies, University of Victoria, 1982). Tromly examines the aesthetic transformation of self-portraiture, seeing Brontë's work not as autobiography cast in fictional form but as fiction cast in autobiographical form.

T. J. Wise and J. A. Symington (eds), *The Brontës: Their lives, friendships and correspondence* (Oxford: Shakespeare Head, 1934). An invaluable collection of letters in which Brontë shows herself to be capable of astute judgment of her own work.

Patricia Yaeger, 'Honey-mad women: Charlotte Brontë's bilingual heroines', *Browning Institute Studies* **14** (1986), pp. 11–35. Yaeger uses the insights of psychoanalysis and deconstruction to provide a symptomatic reading of *Jane Eyre*'s subversive multi-voicedness. She extends that exploration in *Honey-mad women: Emancipatory strategies in women's writing* (New York: Columbia University Press, 1988).

Index

Abbot, Miss, 60, 86
Adams, Maurianne, 26, 28, 105
Adèle, 50–1, 66, 71, 84, 94
Allott, Miriam, 106
Ashe, Frederick, 21
attic, 46
Austen, Jane, 8
authorial identity, 19, 27, 28
antithesis, 19, 20, 23, 24, 35–7,
      39, 61–3, 66–7, 72, 74,
      76,106

Barrett Browning, Elizabeth,
      47, 75
Basch, Françoise, 24
Bayne, Peter, 15
Bellis, Peter, 106
Benevenuto, Richard, 19,
      76, 106
Bessie, 28, 33, 38, 39, 44, 45,
      46, 76, 80
bible, 4, 10
biographical criticism, 14,
      15–16, 18, 19, 20,
      21–2, 106, 107, 108,
      109
Bjork, Harriet, 24
Bloom, Harold, 25
Boumelha, Penny, 28, 63,
      106
Branwell, Aunt, 3, 4

Brocklehurst, Mr, 34, 43, 78,
      79, 87
Brontë, Anne, 5, 10, 12, 15
   Agnes Grey, 10
   The Tenant of Wildfell Hall,
      13
Brontë, Branwell, 10
Brontë, Charlotte
   as author, 3, 5–6, 8, 9, 10–11,
      14, 15, 16, 22, 29,
      107
   critical reception of, 5–6,
      10–11, 12–17, 24,
      54, 75
   as daughter, 4, 5, 6, 29,
      47, 107
   earnings, 5
   education of, 3–4
   as governess, 4, 5
   influences on, 8–10, 96 n10
   Jane Eyre, passim
   juvenilia, 4, 8, 9, 10
   poetry of, 3, 5, 12
   The Professor, 5, 10, 13, 63,
      102 n5
   Shirley, 9, 36, 101–2 n5
   Villette, 3, 14, 36, 62, 78, 79,
      92, 101 n3
   as wife, 6, 7
Brontë, Emily, 5, 10, 12, 15, 16,
      22, 65, 108

Brontë, Emily (*continued*)
   Wuthering Heights, 10, 17, 52,
     65
Brontë, Maria, 47
Brontë, Patrick, 4, 5, 6
Brussels, 3, 5
Bulwer-Lytton, Edward, 10, 14
Bunyan, John, 4, 10
Burns, Helen, 19, 34, 40, 41–2,
     46, 62, 77, 94
Byron, George Gordon, 4, 9

castration, 55, 71, 72
Cecil, Lord David, 16
Chartism, 8, 14
Chase, Karen, 22–3, 82, 83,
     92, 106
Chodorow, Nancy, 36, 37, 47
Cinderella, 37
class, 24, 27, 28, 106, 107
Colby, Vineta, 25
Contratto, Susan, 36
Crompton, D. W., 16

Dale, Peter Allan, 20, 106
deconstruction, 23, 28, 109
Dickinson, Emily, 25
Disraeli, Benjamin, 10, 14
Dooley, Lucile, 21
double standards, 5–6, 13

Eagleton, Terry, 24, 106
economic independence, 4, 5,
     55, 56
education, 4, 8
Ellmann, Mary, 25
Eliot, George, 10, 15, 75, 92
emancipation, 3, 8, 14
employment, 4, 5, 8
Ewbank, Inga-Stina, 25

Fairfax, Mrs, 34, 44, 86
fantasy, 52, 56, 65, 68, 70, 73, 76,
     80, 81, 89, 92, 93, 94, 95

father figure, 39, 68
female suffrage, 8
feminist criticism, 18, 21, 22,
     23, 24–9, 54, 63, 74–5,
     84, 94–5, 105, 106,
     107, 108
feminist movement, 8, 26, 27
film theory, 84, 85, 86, 89, 92,
     104 n21
Forçade, Eugene, 14
formalism, 18, 19, 20
Foucault, Michel, 23

Gaskell, Elizabeth, 6, 9, 13, 14,
     21, 106
Gérin, Winifred, 106
Gilbert, Sandra, 25–6, 27, 61,
     74, 106
Godwin, William, 10
gothic, 9, 21, 107
Grosz, Elizabeth, 36, 47, 51
Gubar, Susan, 25–6, 27, 61,
     74, 106
Gulliver's Travels, 38

Haworth, 4, 5, 10
Heilman, Robert, 9, 21, 107
heroic reading, 28, 56, 74–5,
     76, 78, 83, 84, 89, 93,
     94–5
Homans, Margaret, 29, 107
identity, 41, 49, 58, 59, 68, 72,
     74–92, 93
   divided, 76, 82–3, 89, 90
   retreat from, 89–92, 94
   unified, 28, 74–5, 76, 83,
     84, 90
   unreliability of, 76–83
   unstable, 82, 89
Imaginary, 52, 68, 70, 71, 72,
     92, 94, 95
Ingram, Blanche, 55, 56, 57, 61,
     78, 80, 86
Irigaray, Luce, 36, 47, 68

Index

James, G. P. R., 14

Keefe, Robert, 21–2
Knies, Earl A., 18, 19, 107
Kroeber, Karl, 21,

Lacan, Jacques, 90
Langbridge, Rosamond, 21
law, 7, 8, 14, 28
Leavis, F. R., 16
Lewes, George, 3, 12
Lloyd, Mr, 39
Lytton, *see* Bulwer-Lytton

marriage, 4, 6–7, 8, 57, 58, 59,
    65, 70, 108
Martin, Robert, 18, 19, 107
Martineau, Harriet, 9
Marxist criticism, 18, 21, 23,
    24, 106, 107, 108
Marxist-Feminist literature
    collective, 107
Mason, Bertha, 7, 19, 27–8, 45,
    46, 56, 58, 59–60, 61–
    2, 62–3, 79, 94, 107
Mason, Richard, 77
Maynard, John, 107
Metz, Christian, 86
Mill, John Stuart, 6
Milton, John, 10
mirrors, 49, 69, 70, 91
Moers, Ellen, 25
Moglen, Helene, 21–2, 107
Moi, Toril, 27
motherhood, 25, 33–52, 63, 66,
    67, 72, 76, 89, 90, 92,
    93, 108
    ambivalence toward, 35–7,
        39–40, 42–6, 100 n8
    bad mothers, 35, 38–40, 47,
        49, 69
    dyadic union, 68, 70, 71, 90
    good daughter, 43, 45, 49,
        100 n8

good mothers, 33–5, 39–40,
    47
motherlessness, 47, 48–
    9, 101 n19
    in nature, 34–5, 49
    phallic mother, 36, 47, 52,
        68, 71, 100 n8
    rejection of, 50–1, 89
    and sexuality, 46, 51, 52
Mulvey, Laura, 84

narrative, 40–1, 76–83, 88,
    108
narrative theory, 20, 106
New Criticism, 16, 18, 19,
    20, 23
new historicism, 29
Nicholls, Arthur, 6, 7
Nightingale, Florence, 47, 53
Nussey, Ellen, 8

Oliphant, Margaret, 11, 14

painting, 85–6
Pell, Nancy, 108
Peters, Margot, 20, 108
Pilgrim's Progress, 4
Politi, Jina, 24, 108
Poole, Grace, 28
Poovey, Mary, 23, 29, 108
post–structuralism, 18,19, 23,
    28, 75, 106
psychoanalytic criticism, 18,
    21, 22–3, 24, 75, 108,
    109

racism, 27–8, 63, 106, 108
realism, 9, 12, 23, 28, 108
red-room, 21, 39, 46, 49, 53,
    54, 58
Reed, Eliza, 19
Reed, Georgiana, 19
Reed, John, 19, 40, 53
Reed, Mr, 39

Index

Reed, Mrs, 35, 36, 38, 39, 40,
    44, 45, 46, 48, 49, 51,
    54, 60, 69, 70, 84, 85,
    86, 87
Reid, T. W., 15
Rich, Adrienne, 26, 28, 33, 34,
    35, 75, 108
Richardson, Samuel, 9
Rigby, Elizabeth, 13, 14
Rivers, Diana, 19, 34, 45, 71, 88
Rivers, Mary, 19, 34, 45, 71, 88
Rivers, St John, 19, 34, 35, 49,
    55, 57, 66–7, 70, 77,
    85, 87, 88, 94
Rochester, Edward, 7, 10, 19,
    35, 44, 45, 49, 50, 52,
    55, 56, 57, 58, 61–2,
    63–4, 66, 67–9, 70–4,
    77, 78, 79, 80–1, 83,
    85, 86, 88, 91–2, 94
romanticism, 9
Rosenman, Ellen, 49
Ruskin, John, 6

Said, Edward, 23
Sand, George, 8
Sarraute, Natalie, 41
Scott, Walter, 9
sexism, 6, 7, 13
sexuality, 7, 8, 37, 53–73, 83,
    89, 92, 93
  ambivalence toward, 56
  assertion of, 54–5, 56, 64
  and danger, 57, 58, 64,
    101 n3
  and death, 58–9
  denial of, 53, 61, 62–4
  and dependence, 58, 71–2
  and disgust, 59–61, 64
  equality in, 55–6, 107
  evasion of, 56, 62, 64–5, 66,
    72–3, 89
  and foreignness, 62–4

and fusion, 37, 56, 65, 67–73
and jealousy, 57
and manipulation, 57–8, 64
and violence, 55, 56–7,
    101 n3
Shakespeare, William, 4
Showalter, Elaine, 25, 74, 108
sight, 84–5, 86–9, 90–2,
    103 n20, 106
silence, 41, 90, 93
Smith, Barbara Leigh, 7
Snow White, 37
Southey, Robert, 3
speech, 84–5, 89–90
Spivak, Gayatri, 27–8, 63, 108
Stephen, Leslie, 15–16, 22
structuralism, 18, 20, 22, 23
Swinburne, Algernon, 15
Symbolic Order, 29
Symington, J. A., 109

Tanner, Tony, 20, 84, 89, 108
Tayler, Irene, 22, 108
Taylor, Mary, 8
Temple, Maria, 33–4, 36, 40,
    41–2, 43, 45, 46, 81
Thackeray, William, 6, 9
Tillotson, Geoffrey, 8
Tromly, Annette, 18–19, 20, 22,
    75, 76, 109

Victorian literature, 9, 10, 12,
    13, 23
voyeurism, 87, 91

Ward, Mary, 16
Watts, Isaac, 10
Winnicott, D. W., 49, 69
Wise, T. J., 109
Wooler, Margaret, 3, 5
Woolf, Virginia, 16

Yaeger, Patricia, 28–9, 109